D1449254

THE LONDON THEOLOGICAL LIBRARY

UNDER THE EDITORSHIP OF
THE REV. PROFESSOR ERIC S. WATERHOUSE, M.A., D.D.

THE OLD TESTAMENT
ITS MAKING AND MEANING

D

THE LONDON THEOLOGICAL LIBRARY
Under the Editorship of
THE REV. PROFESSOR ERIC S. WATERHOUSE,
M.A., D.D.

THE
OLD TESTAMENT

ITS MAKING AND MEANING

By

H. WHEELER ROBINSON, M.A., D.D.

Principal of Regent's Park College and
Reader in Biblical Criticism in the
University of Oxford

NASHVILLE — TENNESSEE

COKESBURY PRESS

THE OLD TESTAMENT
ITS MAKING AND MEANING
Copyright MCMXXXVII *— 1937*
By H. Wheeler Robinson

*Set Up, Electrotyped, Printed, and Bound
by the Parthenon Press at Nashville,
Tennessee, United States of America*

C

PREFACE

TECHNICALLY this book belongs to the studies known as "Introduction to the Literature of the Old Testament," which means that it is concerned with "Biblical Criticism" in however elementary a fashion. It seeks to state, in the briefest manner possible, the nature of the thirty-nine books which form our English Old Testament, together with their origins and dates, so far as these can be known. Incidentally, this presupposes a great deal of patient literary analysis, of which the results only can here be given. Such analysis, however, is only a means to an end, that of a better literary, historical, and religious appreciation of the contents of the Old Testament. This, it seems to me, deserves at least as much attention in a book of "Introduction" as the necessary critical analysis; in fact, the truth of the analysis will largely depend on the intrinsic quality of the reconstruction it makes possible. The prejudice of many who are not "obscurantists" against "Biblical Criticism" is that they think this offers but an Ezekielian valley of dry bones over which no breath of the Spirit has blown to re-create human life and exhibit divine grace. The title of the book is meant to suggest this larger interpretation of "introduction"; by the "making" I imply the analytical study of literary origins, and by the "meaning" those qualities of the book which this study reveals the more clearly. I hope that the book is one which the professional student may usefully read as a prelude to more detailed volumes, and the ordinary reader of general education may find sufficient to orientate him and to make the Old Testament more interesting as literature and more inspiring for religion.

The Appendix contains a selection of critical analyses which have proved useful in teaching this subject, and are added for the use of other students; they are not intended for the general reader.

My thanks are due to Professors A. J. D. Farrer and T. H. Robinson for reading the typescript and making useful suggestions, and to Mr. L. H. Brockington for helping in the correction of the proof and for compiling the Index. I am also indebted to Mr. Jonathan Cape for permission to quote the lengthy passage from Doughty's *Arabia Deserta on page* 169.

H. WHEELER ROBINSON.

CONTENTS

7

CONTENTS

CHAPTER IV

CHAPTER V

CHAPTER VI

8

CONTENTS

CHAPTER VII

THE LAW LITERATURE 167

1. The Nature of Early "Law." 2. The Book of the Covenant. 3. The Deuteronomic Laws. 4. The Law of Holiness. 5. The "Legislation" of Ezekiel. 6. The Priestly Law.

CHAPTER VIII

THE CANON 188

1. The Meaning of "Canon." 2. Josiah's Law-book. 3. Ezra's Law-book. 4. The Close of the Pentateuch. 5. The Evidence of Ecclesiasticus. 6. The Close of the Canon. 7. The Present Authority of the Old Testament.

CHAPTER I

THE LIFE BEHIND THE LITERATURE

1. In one of our great libraries there is a manuscript of the Hebrew Bible beautifully written, but having an ugly brown stain on the first and last pages of the Pentateuch. The stain is blood, and in all probability blood shed in some massacre of the Jews and looting of the synagogues. Perhaps it represents the loyalty of a life given in defence of the book. It needs such a loyalty to maintain a religion, but it needs loyalty certainly not less to beget it. The famous words of Milton about great literature are truest of all when they are applied to the literature of the Old Testament—"the precious life-blood of a master spirit, embalmed and treasured up on purpose to a life beyond life."

The literature which constitutes the Old Testament is the slow and largely unconscious deposit of a national life extending over a millennium. That life moved at varying levels of quality, but its finest experiences were gathered up and found classical expression in "master spirits." Some of them are known to us by name, but more are unknown ; and much of their anonymous work gathers round the few remembered names. The anonymity makes no difference to the quality of the product. Known or unknown, it is the life of a people that throbs and pulses through the recorded words.

2. And what a people it is ! The Jew is the standing enigma of the Western world. Despised and hated, persecuted and massacred, repaying his persecutors often enough with a ferocity to match theirs; and yet entering into those thoughts of God which move in a world above all nationalisms and concern the destiny of the whole human race. The characteristics of the people lie before us in the Old Testament literature and in the very qualities of the language in which it is written. It is a language in which every other word is a concealed metaphor, still living to the eye of the scholar, with the sound and colour and movement of its original; a language simple and rugged in its structure, dramatic in its vocabulary, concrete in its expression of even the most spiritual things. There is no room in it for niceties of relation expressed by subordinate conjunctions. The thoughts are flung at you in succession and you are left to relate them for yourself. Such qualities go to make Hebrew one of the two great languages of religion and worthy to match the sonorous Latin. No student of the Hebrew language who comes under its fascination will think it unworthy of the high

thoughts which it struggles to express. There is as much eloquence in its failures as in the success of languages far richer in power of analysis and the expression of subtle relation.

The people who used this language were a people mingled of many racial elements, and their life-blood continued to be fed from many sources; their life itself throughout the centuries of their national co-existence continued to be quickened by many contacts with surrounding peoples. The land in which they lived was eminently suited to be the clearing-house of religion, as a glance at a map of the ancient world-empires will show. It is easy to be wise after the event, and to secure an appearance of divine purpose by eliminating or forgetting all the tentative movements which have not reached fruition. Yet, if we judge the result in the creation of a great literature to be worth while, we are justified in finding the evidence of a divine purpose in this long development of an ancient people. At first open to many external influences, the time came when they had to protect their gains by what may seem to us the shell of a harsh and repellent nationalism; but had they not done this, those gains might have been lost to us.

This was a people which lived intensely, and the more intensely because they believed that they had but one life to live—life upon this visible earth. The apparent simplicity of the universe in Hebrew eyes is well represented by the close of the 115th Psalm. The world is there depicted as a house of three storeys, or let us say two storeys and a basement. The highest level is that of heaven, the solid structure of the firmament, and the heavens are the heavens of the Lord. The basement is Sheol, wherein are those shades, mere ghosts and bloodless replicas of humanity, who have gone down into silence and praise not the Lord. But between the higher and the lower mystery man has the earth as the tenant of God, with the supreme duty of worshipping Him.

This was the people whose great and historic achievement was to create a unique religious literature.

They were not an intellectual people, "sicklied o'er with the pale cast of thought"; their life was emotional and volitional. It covered many interests besides those we should call "religious." Very little secular Hebrew literature of the early days has come down to us, but that wholly secular anthology, the Song of Songs, can fitly suggest to us what the Hebrew could have done, and to some extent did, in literature for its own sake and for its purely æsthetic qualities. But the stern demands of an inscrutable purpose turned the creative passion of the Hebrew into narrower channels that the torrent might rush the more strongly. The peculiar inspiration of the

Hebrew was to be given through his moral and religious interpretation of a richly varied and long-continued history. The gain of such concentration was the conviction, unique in the ancient world, that history was the revelation of God and moved without haste and without rest to His appointed goal; that human society was to be governed by moral standards of mercy and justice and that for this present world and on this present earth, however dark the outlook, it was the darkness before a glorious dawn, that "morning" of the Lord which is so often on the lips of the Psalmists. This is the people whose literature, gathered and edited, written and re-written, purged of some of its ancient features that it might serve new generations, passed to the synagogue of Judaism as the Law, the Prophets, and the Writings, and to the Christian Church as the Old Testament.

3. It is essential to the understanding of this literature that we should always keep in view the history which slowly deposited it. That history is a moving panorama, full of striking contrasts. In the remotest periods we see the Bedouin of the desert very much as Charles Doughty pictured them in his incomparable *Arabia Deserta* (the best of all introductions to the early life of Israel). This was the time when Jacob was a wandering Aramean and when there was no literature, but only that constant prede-

cessor of literature—viz., oral tradition. We dimly see in such of these traditions as have passed into the literature the movements of tribes or clans reflected in stories of individual men and women. We note the drift of ancient Hebrews across the desert and into Palestine and Egypt. There, on its borders, emerges the first figure which we can call historical in the full sense, that of Moses, whose task is to be a patriot and a prophet, delivering these oppressed serfs from the bondage of an alien race and interpreting to them their deliverance as an act of a God known indeed to their ancestors as from afar, but now entering into a new covenanted relation with His people Israel.

Then the scene changes to Canaan, and these nomads, after a period of fierce fighting, pass beneath the influence of a new culture and become agriculturalists. The influence of this relatively high culture of Canaan on the nomadic spirit of the Israelites becomes one of the great motifs in the subsequent religious history, perhaps the most important. From these days comes to us the earliest Hebrew literature, the Song of Deborah, which reminds us that from the outset the rallying cry of the Israelite tribes is "Yahweh," and that its nationalism is itself religious.

When these scattered tribes without political union pass under the rule of the early monarchy, literature in the proper sense begins, and we get such a fine piece of writing as the court history of David, and such interesting light on early customs and ritual as is afforded by the Book of the Covenant.

It is, however, from the eighth to the sixth centuries that we find the golden age of Israel's creative powers in religion. That is the age of the great prophets from Amos to Deutero-Isaiah, with two empires of the ancient world, the Assyrian and the Babylonian, as their background, and indeed more than their background. For it is characteristic of these prophets to claim all the events of history as being in the hand of their God and to interpret that which the secular mind would ascribe to natural causes to one far-reaching divine purpose bending to its will the wills of even the mightiest kings. The first effect of this prophetic work, which characteristically linked morality and religion, is seen in the Book of Deuteronomy, the book which centralized worship in Jerusalem, purged it of its grosser elements, and moralized the content of its ritual. Next came the exile, and by the exile we mean not the period subsequent to the overthrow of the northern kingdom beginning in 722, but that beginning in 586, when the Davidic kingship came to an end after an uninterrupted course of four centuries. The northern exiles are lost to sight; the future was to belong to those from the southern kingdom.

The exile of so many Judeans in Babylonia was both an influence and an opportunity. As an influence it completed the work of the prophets in removing the people from old associations of heathen worship, and at the same time it vindicated the prophetic utterance of judgment and stamped their words with the seal of truth. As an opportunity it was of the first importance for the gathering and editing of the extant literature, indeed, for its preservation. It is when we run the risk of losing things that we are most likely to value them, and it was the very loss of so many of the past privileges that made thoughtful and religious men cherish with the greater zeal the written records of them and extend and revise the story of past happenings, written or unwritten, in the light of the exile itself. This was the age in which the law codes, subsequent to Deuteronomy, began to be written down and shaped into their present form, whilst the prophetic "words" were no less zealously collected.

The period subsequent to the return of certain of the exiles and their reanimation of the religious life of those who had never been exiled shows entirely new conditions. We have now a religious community rather than a nation, existing by grace of a foreign power and with no political independence, and centred in the Temple and its worship. This is the period in which many of the psalms must have been written, though others had come down as a heritage from the pre-exilic days. There are certain will-lit spots on the road traversed by these centuries, such as the rebuilding of the Temple, described in Haggai and Zechariah, and the rebuilding of the walls described in Nehemiah; but darkness has fallen on most of the period, so far as its outward and visible course is concerned. It was, however, rich in literary productivity, and to it belonged the Wisdom literature of Israel, including the most brilliant piece of literature in the Old Testament, the Book of Job. The Persian empire gave place to that of the Greeks, and in the long struggle between Seleucids and Ptolemies the land of Palestine was an easy prey for either combatant till the national life revived again with the Maccabees and their successors, the Hasmoneans. This is the age in which apocalyptic literature begins; of this the Book of Daniel in its later portions is the best-known Old Testament example. Apocalyptic is the most direct descendant of the prophetic literature and has indeed been defined as unfulfilled prophecy. In spite of all its vagaries as judged by our modern and Western standards, Apocalyptic does set forth in most emphatic fashion that hope of Israel which was to reach nobler and purer forms through faith in the Christian Messiah.

4. The literary products of this long historical development lie before us in the Old Testament, not in their chronological order, but as edited, rearranged, and revised for a specific purpose. It is the task of that literary criticism which constitutes "introduction" in the technical sense, to penetrate these later forms and discover the historical order and original significance of the literature so far as this is possible. In its present form, as shaped by the later post-exile Judaism, the Old Testament falls into three distinct portions—namely, the Law, the Prophets, and the Writings. The "Law"—that is, the Pentateuch—is of very composite character. It contains the early traditions as written down from, say, the ninth century B.C., ancient songs and customs, priestly rules, sermons, formal and spontaneous narratives. The "Prophets" include for the Jew what we call historical books—viz., Joshua, Judges, 1 and 2 Samuel, and 1 and 2 Kings. The "Prophets" in our more limited sense are as literature the collection and expansion of spoken oracles, usually but not exclusively consisting of brief and detached units. These have been collected largely by disciples of the prophets without much regard to their order and on no systematic plan of topics, so that the authorship and date and sometimes even the meaning of a particular paragraph is open to question. The prophetic oracles were col-

lected in four great rolls, which came to bear the names of Isaiah, Jeremiah, Ezekiel, and "the Twelve." But it was a matter of convenience or superficial association rather than literary judgment which must often have decided on what roll a particular prophecy was written. The third portion of the Hebrew Old Testament is known as the "Writings" and contains the Psalms, Proverbs, and Job, a group of five books known as "the Rolls" (Megilloth), Daniel, Ezra, Nehemiah, and Chronicles (in this order).

We see then that the Old Testament as it lies before us consists of Hebrew literature selected and rearranged to make a religious book, though it should be noted that the Bible of Judaism is essentially the Law or Torah, to which the Prophets and the Writings are subordinate. The present arrangement conveys the belief that Israel's national history began with the giving of the Torah and that the Prophets were necessary only because people neglected the Torah. These and other Jewish theories, however interesting and valuable as part of the history of the people, must be resolutely set aside where honest literary criticism demands it. The outstanding theological belief of the present arrangement of the Old Testament is that of faith in a divine election, enshrined and expressed in the Covenant which from time to time Yahweh made with His people. Historically this faith in its simplest form goes back in all probability to Moses and the Exodus, but it was the Prophets who first emphasized it and made it the very backbone of Israel's religion. How different were the earlier historical facts from the later interpretations may be seen by comparing the books of Samuel and Kings with the ecclesiastical version of the same events which we have in Chronicles. But it is unavoidable that later generations using a remote literature as part of their religious inheritance should reinterpret and transform the meaning of the events, if not the events themselves; we may compare the later, allegorical moralizing of Homer. This Jewish reinterpretation is embedded in the Old Testament itself. The Christian reinterpretation is seen in the writings of the New Testament, and the history of exegesis through the Christian centuries shows us that the process is ceaseless. It is indeed a necessary process for any book which is regarded as the oracles of a living God. Our purpose in this volume is not to study this religious and theological development, nor to trace the history of the Bible in the Church. It is our task to lay the foundation for the study of both the history and the religion of Israel by a study of the books of the Old Testament interpreted so far as possible as literature, and in their original (historical) setting.

CHAPTER II

THE BEGINNINGS OF THE LITERATURE

Wherever we can trace the beginnings of a native literature, it springs from an oral tradition, a saying or a song, a tale or a formula passed on from mouth to ear, often through many generations before it was recorded by the artificial aid of writing. Thus Professor Gilbert Murray, in tracing *The Rise of the Greek Epic*, says that "Greek saga was mainly preserved by oral tradition . . . all through antiquity a book remained a thing to be recited from, or to be read aloud to an audience by a skilled person" (pp. 94, 95n.). Perhaps nowhere can the process be better illustrated than from Arabia, where the historical conditions for the rise of a literature came very late, and where the unlettered Bedouin of modern times offers so precise a parallel to his ancestors of a remote past. Doughty met a sheikh who "told me upon his fingers his twelve homeborn ancestors; this is nearly four centuries" (*Arabia Deserta*, I, p. 126). We can easily imagine how many fragments of ancient tradition would be fitted, with more or less accuracy, into such a framework. The material would inevitably be remoulded and refashioned, contracting and expand-

23

ing from generation to generation; but the very nature of the process ensured the emergence of some of the qualities that make literature, if not the data for history—the choice of the fitting word, the retention of essentials, the concrete presentation of life. On the same page, Doughty writes of listening for hours to a teller of tales, "all of good matter and eloquent, and (as unlettered men tell) of the marrow of human experience," whilst elsewhere (I, p. 388) he illustrates the fact that such oral tradition frequently avails itself of poetic form (which is so much more easily remembered than prose) : "The lays of the B. Helál are chanted in every wild hamlet of worsted booths, in the immeasurable wilderness—an unwritten scripture (which moves the younger sort) of the ostentation of liberality, and the prowess in the field."

In such ways, and of similar substance, Israel's literature began to be. The nomad Israelites brought with them from the desert many fragments of their oral tradition, some of which can still be recognized as embedded in their later literature. Thus the "Song of the Well" (Num. xxi. 17, 18) is an ancient adjuration of some ancestral spring that it may give an ample supply of water, a custom paralleled by the songs of modern Bedouin when they draw water for their flocks. "The Book of Jashar," to which reference is made in Joshua x. 13, 2 Sam. i. 18, and 1 Kings

viii. 53 (LXX), seems to have been an anthology of heroic deeds and notable events and sayings—something like the "Hamasa" collected by an early Arabian poet from surviving Arabic verse, and including songs of heroes, laments for the dead, aphorisms, love songs, taunts, songs of hospitality and honour, etc. Another illustration of such songs is that of Lamech (Gen. iv. 23, 24).

One important line of such early tradition can be seen in the tribal songs, which are now found collected in "The Blessing of Jacob" (Gen. xlix) and "The Blessing of Moses" (Deut. xxxiii). A poem still earlier as a unity is "The Song of Deborah" (Judges v), probably the earliest piece of "literary" composition which the Old Testament contains, and one that doubtless had a long oral transmission before it took written form.

Early stories, not in poetic form, are illustrated by those of Abraham's superhuman visitors (Gen. xviii), or Isaac's marriage (Gen. xxiv), or Jacob's cunning (Gen. xxx). Sometimes these stories would explain an important change of custom, as does that of Abraham's intended sacrifice of Isaac (Gen. xxii) ; or they might explain the origin of a neighbouring people, such as the Ammonites and the Moabites—hated kinsfolk of Israel (Gen. xix. 30 ff.)—or the story might

be linked to a sanctuary, like that of Jacob at Bethel
(Gen. xxviii).

The traditions of local sanctuaries must have
been an important element in the chain of pre-literary
transmission. They would include not only instructions as to ritual but also oracles given to enquirers,
which would tend to become precedents. From such
sources, rather than from formal legislation, the important law-codes of the Old Testament have
emerged (see Ch. VII). The content of such local
(Canaanite) traditions would naturally be taken over
by the Israelites as they gradually became the dominant element in Canaan; but we must also allow for
the nomadic tradition which they brought with them
from the desert (cf. Ex. xviii for legal decisions).

Another element in the material of oral tradition
was undoubtedly the wise or witty saying, epitomiz-
ing the popular ideal of sagacity, and memorable from
its form. Under this head come the riddles and sayings of Samson (Judges xiv. 14, 18, xv. 16) and the
fable of Jotham (Judges ix. 8 ff.). From such material developed in due course the "Wisdom" literature
of Israel (see Ch. VI).

One more oral contribution, and this of the
highest importance, is the prophetic oracle, as distinct
from the priestly oracle, given at a sanctuary or
through the casting of lots). The earliest known

Canaanite instance of this occurred at Byblos about 1100 B.C., when a page of the prince was seized with an ecstatic frenzy during the offering of sacrifice, and uttered an oracle which the prince obeyed (Erman, *Literature of the Ancient Egyptians*, Eng. Trans., p. 177). It is possible that this phenomenon of ecstatic prophecy was derived from the Canaanites by the Hebrews; it is seen in the early *Nebi'im*, in the time of Samuel, who was in close touch with them (1 Sam. x. 5 ff.) and shared their experience (xix. 20 ff.). Gradually the emphasis shifted from the psycho-physical phenomena to the moral and spiritual content of the oracle, though something of the former belonged to all the prophets, even the greatest (e.g., Isa. viii. 11, xx. 2, 3; Jer. xx. 9; Ezek. iii. 14, 15). The earliest oracles were probably short and enigmatic, or at least symbolic in form; they often challenged attention by their obscurity, and would be repeated and remembered by the prophet's followers and disciples, till they took shape as a written collection of his utterances. It is a long journey from Micaiah's vision of the heavenly council (1 Kings xxii. 19) to the autobiographic poems and denunciatory "sermons" of the prophet Jeremiah; but its accompaniment is chiefly oral, not written, tradition, which explains many of the difficulties of the exegete. In fact, we can see in Isa. viii. 16 and Jer. xxxvi. 2 ff. how the oracles, given by mouth and treasured by memory alone, came at last to be written down.

Along such lines of development as this the main types of literature in the Old Testament have come into being. Five of these lines will have to be traced —viz., History, Prophecy, Psalms, Wisdom, and Law. Of these five, the second, as will be seen, became the dominant element in moulding the religion and controlling the literary record of it. The story of the development along these five lines provides a virtual "Introduction" to the Old Testament, with the advantage that we are more likely to be conscious of the dynamic element and progressive movement which are so characteristic of this book. It cannot too often be asserted that the revelation of Israel's living God is in the dynamic movement of history; from the beginning and throughout most of the course of that history the written record held a quite subsidiary place.

Moreover, it must not be forgotten that a large part, and that the most important part, of the literature is poetry and not prose. This applies not only to those books, or parts of books, which the R. V. prints as poetry—Job, Psalms, Proverbs, Canticles—but to the chief elements in the prophets, where the parallelism and the rhythmical stress are often obscured by their being printed as prose. [Of these two features of Hebrew poetry, the parallelism is the more important for exegesis; it consists in the varied repetition (synthetic or antithetic) of the same thought, or in its balanced continuation, seen in such a saying as:

> *The Lord knoweth the way of the righteous:*
> *But the way of the wicked shall perish* (Ps. i. 6).]

Fortunately, the parallelism and to some extent the rhythm can usually be recognized, even when set out as prose in the English version. Together with the poetic vocabulary of the prophets, it should serve to remind us that the "living oracles" of God claimed the music of poetry as their characteristic mode of utterance. Because this has been forgotten, they have often, like their human utterers, been wounded in the house of their friends. Poetry, like prayer, is apt to fare ill on the Procrustean bed of dogma. If prayer be, as Wellhausen said, the only adequate confession of faith, we might almost dare to say that poetry is the only adequate revelation of divine truth.

Finally, we should note that the literature which began as oral tradition had its days "bound each to each by natural piety." For the most part, it still bears the stamp of the spoken and not written word. Indeed, its very circulation even when written depended on the mouth and the ear far more than on the eye. We must go behind, not only the printed book in the hands of the modern man, but also the manuscript itself, rare and accessible to, and readable by, a very small minority. True, the public reading of the Law in the synagogues (not in the Temple) eventually made it familiar to the devout worshipper. This, however, belonged to a relatively late stage of the religion of the Old Testament; it is not until the Maccabean age that we have evidence of a "book" religion. As we read the literature of the Old Testament, therefore, we do well to remind ourselves constantly that its stories were made to be told, its psalms to be sung, its oracles to be spoken with authority, its laws to be the memoranda of the authorities in a court of appeal. No book mediated the religion of Israel until its most creative period was past. To think of this fact will urge us the more to listen for what Sir George Adam Smith has happily called "the sound of running history," and so better to understand the literature that was the record, long before it became the creator, of living religion.

NOTE ON WRITING AND WRITING MATERIALS

The emphasis which has been laid on oral transmission in this chapter does not spring from any neglect of *the existence of writing* in Palestine from an early date. That writing was practised in Palestine before the fifteenth century B.C. is clear from its copious use in the Amarna

Age. This writing, however, was in the Babylonian cuneiform, which combines signs denoting syllables, such as *ab, ba,* and signs representing an idea, such as *sarru,* "king." There are no simple consonantal and vowel signs, as in our alphabet. The Semite peoples of Canaan, however, employed an alphabet of twenty-two letters, from which that of the Greeks and of other nations of Europe was derived through the Phœnicians. This alphabet is employed on a Phœnician tomb (Ahiram) of the eleventh century or possibly earlier, on the Moabite Stone of the ninth century, and on the Hebrew ostraka of Samaria of the same century. Its origin is not known, but the recent discovery of a probably alphabetic (cuneiform) script at Ras Shamra suggests that the Phœnicians are the most likely people to have invented it, possibly by development from Babylonian or Egyptian signs. The Hebrews learnt it, we may suppose, from their Canaanite neighbors, with so many other elements of their culture; but at what date we cannot say. There is an agricultural calendar found at Gezer in Hebrew writing, which may be a little earlier even than the ostraka; it has been dated at 900 B.C. (Jack, *Samaria in Ahab's Time,* p. 44). Gideon is said to have captured a young man of Succoth, who wrote down for him a list of the leading people (Judges viii. 14, R. V. *mar.*). There is no reason, at any rate, to doubt that there were Hebrews able to write by the time that there was likely to be any demand for writing. So far as anything we can call literature is concerned, this would not be before the settled conditions of David's time gave men leisure and inclination to write.

The writing materials of the Hebrews were not the

moist clay and the wedge-shaped stylus of the Babylonians, but either prepared skins of animals, such as were employed for the Torah-rolls at a later date, or the papyrus. That papyrus was used in Palestine at an early date may be seen from the fact that about the year 1100 Wenamon brought 500 rolls of papyrus from Egypt for the king of Gebal. The roll on which Baruch wrote at the dictation of Jeremiah in 604 was probably a roll of papyrus, rather than leather, on which the scribe wrote with a reed pen in ink (some dark fluid) and in columns or "doors"; when three or four of these columns had been read, the angry king slashed them off with the scribe's penknife, and threw them into the brazier (Jer. xxxvi. 23). Such writing could be washed off with water, as we see in the ordeal of jealousy (Num. v. 23). Moses is represented as saying (Ex. xxxii. 32), "Wipe me from thy book." The scribe carried an inkhorn at his belt (Ezek. ix. 2), as well as the knife for trimming the reed pen. The writing could be kept in earthenware vessels, like the deeds of Jeremiah's property at Anathoth (Jer. xxxii. 14). Tablets of harder material were also used, such as stone (on which the decalogue was engraved) or metal, when an iron stylus would be used (cf. Job xix. 24; Jer. xvii. 1). Ezekiel (iv. 1) draws a representation of Jerusalem on a clay tile or brick, and the use of potsherds as account books has been made familiar to us from the excavations at Samaria. The ordinary writing ("with the pen of a man") used by Isaiah would be like the writing of the contemporary Siloam inscription.

CHAPTER III

HISTORY

1. Not only is the literature constituting the Old Testament a gradual deposit from Israel's history, but the Old Testament itself largely takes the form of historical narrative. This is as it should be, for one of the great contributions made by Israel is the conception of the unity of history as controlled by divine purpose. This conception was first fashioned through the prophets' interpretations of contemporary events. It found more formal utterance in the apocalyptic visions of Daniel concerning the kingdom of God, and through Christianity it entered into the stock of general ideas. Born of religion, it loses its grasp on our minds with the decline of religion. This is reflected in the present-day medley of views concerning the principles of history, whilst the contemporary interest in a philosophy of history is a healthy sign of reaction from these uncertainties.

The historical books of the Old Testament may be discussed in three groups, together with an appendix of three short stories—namely, Esther, Ruth, and Jonah. The first group is the Pentateuch. In substance, of course, this is predominantly legal in character and will be discussed in Chapter VII. But in present form the Pentateuch is a history of mankind from the creation to the death of Moses, the great prophet of God, through whom a number of codes of divine law are represented as being given. History, in fact, within the Pentateuch is made a framework for the legislation.

A second group consists of the four books classified in the Hebrew Bible as "The Former Prophets"—namely, Joshua, Judges, 1 and 2 Samuel, 1 and 2 Kings. These present a more or less continuous story of Israel's fortunes from the death of Moses down to the destruction of Jerusalem in 586 B.C. The third group consists of the work of the Chronicler—namely, 1 and 2 Chronicles, Ezra, and Nehemiah; whilst the two latter contain earlier documents, the impress of the Chronicler's work on the whole of these books creates a unity. The earlier history is thus rewritten from Adam down to the foundation of Judaism in the post-exilic period. The interest is ecclesiastical, and earlier statements, such as are found in 1 and 2 Samuel and 1 and 2 Kings, are revised and edited in this interest. Altogether, it will be seen, we have the framework of history from the beginning of the world down to about 400 B.C., though, of course, with many lacunæ.

2. It is necessary to remind ourselves at the be-

ginning that the modern way of writing history is very different from the ancient. The science of history as practised to-day aims at a continuous and self-consistent reconstruction of the past on the basis of its surviving documents. It aims also at an impartial interpretation of the events, though the attitude of the historian will always, at least implicitly, affect his reconstruction. On the other hand, Hebrew writers of history adopted a patchwork or scrapbook method, wherever possible. They pieced together the records they possessed, doing only such editorial work upon them as their purpose required. This purpose, however, was usually made explicit. Without any developed sense of historical perspective they interpreted the past by conditions contemporary with themselves. This led, as we shall see from the work of the Chronicler in particular, to a freedom in writing the history of the past which led to quite unhistorical results. The school of writers who are called "Deuteronomistic" (see p. 59), whilst summarizing the events of the past in a form nearer to their actual happening, did not hesitate to set them in a framework of theory—e.g., the doctrine of divine retribution, which also led to unhistoric results. We must not forget, however, that Hebrew writers often show evident delight in storytelling for its own sake, in addition to any purpose they cherished. This may be seen in some of the patriarchal narratives, or in the stories of early kings and prophets.

3. *The Pentateuch.* The name Pentateuch, derived from the Greek, denotes the "five-roll" book. The corresponding Jewish name is "the five-fifths of the Law" because it was written on five rolls. The familiar titles, Genesis, Exodus, etc., are reproduced from the names given in the Greek version, known as the Septuagint (the division into five books had then already been made, though it does not correspond with the original elements of which the Pentateuch is composed). Let us glance through the Pentateuch as it lies before the English reader in order to give its general plan before we turn to what critical analysis reveals.

The book of Genesis in its present form consists of (1) an account of the primeval world, culminating in the genealogy and place of Abraham amongst the peoples of the East (cc. i-xi). (2) The story of Abraham and to a small degree that of Isaac (cc. xii-xxvi). (3) Jacob (cc. xxvii-xxxvi). (4) Joseph (cc. xxxvii-l).

Thus the three generations, Abraham, Isaac, and Jacob, are succeeded by the important figure of Joseph, as the link with the life of the people in Egypt. A noticeable feature throughout the book is the successive concentration on a particular figure, whilst

36

side-lines of development (Ishmael, Esau) are noticed and dismissed. The primary interest, then, is to trace the Israelites back to their beginnings in the most remote past, and the story naturally expands in detail as we descend. Another important feature is that tribal history is often recounted through the adventures of its ancestors, so that it is very difficult to draw the line between what should be interpreted as tribal and what as individual. We may say then that the object of Genesis is to trace Israel's ancestry, privileges, and possessions. The narrative culminates in the death of Joseph, and in the Book of Exodus we pass from family to national history.

The Book of Exodus is divided by its subject-matter into three parts: (1) Israel's fortunes in Egypt (cc. i–xv. 21). (2) The journey from Egypt to Sinai (cc. xv. 22–xviii. 27). (3) Events occurring at Sinai, and in particular the making of the Covenant between Yahweh and Israel, followed by the erection of the tabernacle.

The Book of Leviticus contains hardly any narrative and is a collection of legal rules dealing chiefly with sacrifice and the work of the priests. The title "Leviticus" is misleading, since the book is concerned largely with the priests and not at all with the Levites. An account of the chief forms of sacrifice (i-v) is followed by further sacrificial rules (vi-vii) and the order for the consecration and induction of priests (viii-x). Then follow rules about the division between clean and unclean and the account of the Day of Atonement, in which the first half of the book culminates (xi-xvi). The second half of the book, which has come to be called by scholars the "Law of Holiness," appears to be an independent body of legislation (xvii-xxvi), whilst the closing chapter (xxvii) is an appendix dealing with vows and their redemption. The Book of Numbers resumes the narrative form, and its first ten chapters deal with the census, the camp, the Levites and their services, the unclean, Nazarites, offerings and leaders, Passover rules, the Pillars of Cloud and of Fire, and the Silver Trumpets. These may be roughly grouped as final arrangements before Sinai is left, whilst a second part of the book (x. 11–xxii. 1) traces the fortunes of Israel in its journeyings from Sinai to Moab, and the third division of the book (xxii. 2–xxxvi) covers events happening and laws given in Moab. Thus the book, in spite of very varied contents, brings Israel to the threshold of the promised land.

The fifth book of the Pentateuch—namely, Deuteronomy—is of a character quite different from the rest. In form it consists of several addresses delivered to the Israelites by Moses in the land of Moab. The first (i. 6–iv. 40) is a historical review of Israel's fortunes since the sacred mountain was left, concluding with a peroration. The second and main address of Moses (v. ff.) begins with the Decalogue as given at Horeb (the name given to Sinai in this book), and urges the oneness of God, as against the many Baalim, through what has become the great Jewish confession of faith, "Hear, O Israel" (vi. 4-9), which holds a place corresponding with the Lord's Prayer of the Christians and the "Faticha" or opening chapter of the Kuran. The nations of Canaan are to be destroyed, and prosperity will depend on strict obedience. Yahweh is punishing the Canaanites for their wickedness rather than rewarding Israel for its merit. In ch. xi, choice is offered of a blessing or a curse according as Israel shall be obedient or disobedient. So far, then, we have a moral and religious introduction to the legislation which follows in cc. xii-xxvi, closing with a renewed appeal for obedience and loyalty. Further addresses are recorded in xxvii-xxx, whilst the last portion of the book, xxxi-xxxiv, gives an account of the closing days of Moses and includes two poems, the Song of xxxii and the Blessing of xxxiii, which are ascribed to him. The Pentateuch fitly closes with the death of Moses on Mount Pisgah (xxxiv). He has brought Israel to a new beginning in which he may not himself share, though Jewish fancy in its later comments has described how God gave him in panoramic vision the history of the successive generations in Palestine—a history to which his work was the prelude both in its religious and political aspect.

The Literary Sources. The outline of the Pentateuch given above takes it at its face value—i.e., as a history containing legislation and unified by a single purpose. But attentive reading prepares us to believe that the unity has been imposed on material of very different kinds, and did not belong originally to this material. The vivid stories of Genesis, the legislative rules of Leviticus, and the rhetorical speech of the first half of Deuteronomy are felt to be quite different in style, even in the English Versions. Closer study reveals a number of repetitions and inconsistencies which make it difficult to think that the Pentateuch has been written by a single author. Such are, for example, the two quite different accounts of the creation in Genesis i and ii, the two accounts of Joseph's removal to Egypt, in one of which Reuben and the Midianites, and in the other Judah and the Ishmaelites are the instruments (Gen. xxxvii. 22 ff.), the way in which a new code of laws begin in Leviticus xvii, without regard to what has preceded it, such manifest contradictions as the statements that all Levites are priests (Deut. xviii. 1) and that only Aaronites are priests (Lev. i. 5). Such details as these are very numerous, and suggest that we are dealing with documents written by various authors at different periods, which have subsequently been edited and combined into a single work. The clue to this "Documentary Theory" (which still holds the field as the best explanation of the phenomena) was given by the use of different divine names, without adequate reason for the difference. Thus in Genesis i the name "Elohim" is used, and in Genesis ii the name "Yahweh" (represented by capital letters in the R. V. as "LORD"). This alone would not be sufficient to distinguish the documents, because names might sometimes be interchanged by revision or by scribal accident, as the Greek Version suggests. But it is the nature of a clue to lead us to further evidence rather than to be complete in itself. The use of this clue was facilitated by the statement of one writer, in Exodus iii. 13-15, that the name "Yahweh" was then revealed to Moses for the first time, and by the parallel statement, apparently of another writer, in Exodus vi. 3, that God was not known to Abraham, Isaac, and Jacob by the name Yahweh, but as El Shaddai (R. V. *mar.*). We can therefore be confident that the writer who uses the name Yahweh from the beginning (Gen. ii) and expressly states that it was used from the time of Adam's grandson (Gen. iv. 26) cannot be the same as the two writers who say in their different ways that it was not so used. By the use, then, of such evidence as this, partly linguistic and partly from subject-matter, it has proved possible to analyse the Pentateuch into four principal sources, conveniently known as J, E, D, and P. The first, which uses the name Yahweh (Jehovah) from Genesis ii onwards, seems to have belonged to the southern group of tribes and to be more concerned with southern places, such as Hebron and the Dead Sea. To this source we owe the simple and unaffected anthropomorphism, such as represents Yahweh as walking in the garden to enjoy the cool of the day. The second, using the name Elohim prior to Exodus iii. 13, and known as E, seems to have sprung from the northern tribal groups, and shows interest in Bethel and Shechem. There is less anthropomorphism in the narrative of this source, which seems to have begun from Abraham, whom God called from a heathen environment (Joshua xxiv. 2, 3). These two sources are usually dated (as literary compositions) from about 850 and 750 B.C. respectively. They seem to have been combined into a single story before they were incorporated into the Pentateuch, and it is often impossible to separate them with confidence. They stand together in sharp contrast to the latest of the four sources—viz., P, denoting the "Priestly" narrative, beginning in Genesis i. The

differences of P are partly due to formalism of style
and a strongly marked vocabulary, which of course
is much less apparent in the English than in the
Hebrew, and partly to the interest of this source in
genealogies, priestly claims and ceremonies, exact
chronology and measurements—all of which combine
to give a very different effect from the simply told
and highly picturesque stories of JE. In fact, the
ordinary reader might almost make a working division
of JE from P by selecting all those portions of Genesis,
Exodus, and Numbers which most appealed to him.
(Leviticus is wholly priestly though including more
than one law-code.) This priestly narrative, which
has been formally expanded to enormous length at
special points through the introduction of the various
priestly codes subsequently inserted in it, is supposed
to have been begun during the exile, and is roughly
dated about 500 B.C.

This leaves us with the fourth source, the Book
of Deuteronomy (to xxxi. 13) known as D. The
central part of this is identified by most scholars with
the lawbook which Josiah made the basis of his reformation of religion in 621 B.C. (2 Kings xxii, xxiii).
The style of Deuteronomy, seen particularly in the
series of "introductions" to the legislation proper,
which follows from xii onwards, is not less characteristic than that of the priestly writers. The influence

of its teaching was very great, as we shall see from the editing of earlier material in the light of its principles which is found in other books. The date of Deuteronomy is therefore an important one for Biblical criticism, for much turns on it in regard to the dating of other books. In spite of attempts to put it either earlier or later, the majority of scholars are still convinced that the central part, at least, of our Deuteronomy figured in the Josianic Reformation (see Ch. VII, pp. 178 ff.).

In regard to the linguistic style of Deuteronomy, upwards of seventy characteristic usages have been collected (as by Driver, *Commentary,* pp. lxxvii ff.). Many of these can easily be noticed by the reader of the English Bible, because of their frequent repetition —e.g., "a mighty hand and a stretched out arm," "with all thy heart and with all thy soul," "as at this day," "as the LORD hath spoken (i.e., promised)," references to the divine choice of Israel, or to the prolonging of Israel's days. The general difference of the rhetorical and expansive expression of the thought from the simpler and terser languages of JE will be obvious.

There is a corresponding difference of outlook shown in a large number of details, from the rest of the Pentateuch, whether it be the earlier (JE) or the later (P) portions. For example, in Exodus xxi.

13, 14 (JE), the altars of Yahweh, wherever found, provide sanctuary for the man who has killed another without intent, whereas in Deuteronomy xix (such altars apart from Jerusalem having been abolished by the legislation of the book) three "cities of refuge" are provided for this purpose. In Deuteronomy xviii. 3, the priests' due in a peace-offering is a shoulder, the two cheeks, and the maw, but in Leviticus vii. 32-34 (P), it is the right thigh and the breast, showing the natural tendency for the priestly perquisites to increase in value.

The Value of the Pentateuch. It is not necessary to estimate separately the five books of the Pentateuch, because as such none of them had separate existence in the course of their making, apart from their nucleus, Deuteronomy, which is noticed farther on. Moreover, we are concerned in this chapter with the historical and not the legislative parts of the Pentateuch, which belong to Ch. VII. The value of the rest of the Pentateuch may be sufficiently suggested by glancing at (*a*) the primeval mythology, (*b*) the patriarchal legends, (*c*) the Exodus and its central figure, (*d*) the religion of Deuteronomy, (*e*) the conception of the priestly history. Around these themes, the reader of the English Bible may conveniently gather the fruits of his own reading of it, which nothing can replace.

(*a*) The early stories contained in Genesis ii-xi are strictly "myths," partly drawn from Babylonian mythology. They belong fundamentally to that large class of stories which attempt to explain the origin of things, so that in one sense they are the science as well as the history of a people's childhood. Why does man wear clothes? why does he sometimes wander about instead of living a settled life? why do not all men speak the same language? why must they work for their living? why is childbirth painful? and so on. The answers are given in the stories of Adam and Eve, Cain, the tower of Babel, etc. To us, they may seem childish enough, considered as answers to these questions, for they were given by those who were but children in relation to ourselves, as we shall doubtless seem to those who come after us. Prior to the rise of conceptual thinking and abstract terminology there can be no explanation of origins save in the concrete form of the story. But to these old tales, which perhaps mostly came down through the Canaanites to the Hebrews, the people of Yahweh added the little more which is so much—faith in their God as controlling the course of events, so that neither man nor giant can defy Him, nor tower of Babel storm His heavenly dwelling, and a moral consciousness which has made the story of the Temptation and Fall of man a parable of truth for all generations.

(*b*) The stories of the patriarchs are to be classed as "legends" rather than "myths." They have doubtless gathered round real persons, or there have been real persons corresponding to those portrayed, though these stories have been so much transformed in oral transmission that we cannot treat them as history. They reflect history; for such stories of individual men often recounted tribal and clan movements and fortunes, as they do still in the tales of the nomads. The story of Abraham's nephew, Lot, for example, and of his daughter's incest (Gen. xix. 30 ff.) expresses at once Israel's sense of kinship with Moabites and Ammonites, as sprung from this incest, and their dislike and hostility towards these peoples. Ishmael explains the Bedouin of the desert, Esau the Edomites of the south. The supremacy of Joseph in Egypt, perhaps connected with the tradition of the invasion of Egypt by the Hyksos, points to the supremacy of the Joseph-clans in the later history; the twelve sons of Jacob are a genealogical explanation of what were ultimately regarded as the twelve tribes of Israel, an artificial creation to explain the varied elements of which the nation found itself to be composed. The easy transition from individual to tribe may be illustrated from Genesis x. 15, where Canaan, here represented as a grandson of Noah, "begat Zidon his first-born and Heth," Zidon being a city and Heth a people.

Excavations at Samaria have recently yielded a number of place-names which are given genealogically in Joshua xvii. 2, 3; the compiler has turned the names of places into those of ancestors, masculine place-names being made into male ancestors and feminine into female ancestors.

But there is a high religious value in these patriarchal stories quite apart from the degree to which they reflect history. They are the concrete embodiment of moral and religious ideals, not always those of ourselves (cf. Abraham's lying in Gen. xii. 13, which is so repugnant to our more developed moral sense), yet often true for morality and religion through all the generations (cf. Esau's generosity to Jacob and Abraham's intercession for righteous men in Sodom). The portrait of Abraham, elsewhere called the friend of God (2 Chron. xx. 7; Isa. xli. 8; Jas. ii. 23) is a fine picture of the meaning of fellowship with God, and the fruit of such a fellowship is strikingly depicted in the story of the sacrifice of Isaac. The divine providence stands out in the story of Joseph, characteristically recounted at such length. Some of the national characteristics are portrayed in the story of the wandering Aramean, Jacob (Deut. xxvi. 5). The literary beauty of many of the stories needs no emphasis; it is sufficient to read the narrative of the marriage of Rebecca in Genesis xxiv. The permanent and yet many-sided appeal of such a story as Jacob's struggle in the darkness (Gen. xxxii. 24 ff.), which may go back to the myth of a river-demon jealous of all who cross his waters, is seen in the fact that the Hebrew form of the story, referring it to Yahweh, uses it to explain the new name and divine blessing of the people of Israel, whilst Hosea (xii. 4, 5) can make it a type of persistency in prayer. Jacob's discovery of a friend in the disguise of a foe is a suggestive parallel to the re-interpretation of the sufferings of the exile in Isaiah liii.

(c) The outstanding historical event of the history of Israel is disclosed in the Pentateuch is undoubtedly the Exodus, which became for the later Israel the signal example of Yahweh's "salvation," and the ground for constantly renewed hope. Here we have the first great example of the mere event transformed by the faith of a prophet into a "fact" for religion. We may only conjecture what "natural" causes have lain behind Israel's deliverance from Egypt; the essential thing is that Moses was there to interpret them. He ranks with the prophets from his call (Ex. iii) onwards, though he is represented as standing in a relation to God closer than that of any prophet (Num. xii. 6 ff.). So he can be the great intercessor (Ex. xxxii. 11, 31 ff., xxxiii. 13 ff., xxxiv. 9; Num. xi. 11 ff., xiv. 13 ff.; cf. Ex. xvii. 11). Besides his general leadership, he is also the nomadic sheikh (Ex. xviii. 13 ff.) round whose name the legislation of many centuries is destined to gather. Perhaps nowhere is the magnanimity of Moses more strikingly displayed than in the story of primitive "prophesying" (see Ch. IV), in which he is represented as saying to Joshua, jealous of his leader's privilege, "Would God that all Yahweh's people were prophets, that Yahweh would put his Spirit upon them!" Who does not feel the pathos of the Pisgah-vision (Deut. xxxiv. 1-6)? Yet how true it is to our human history that the patriot whose heart was first stirred by the sight of injustice to his people (Ex. ii. 11 ff.) should bear the burden of their iniquity, in losing the consummation of his desire (Deut. i. 37, iv. 21, 22).

(*d*) The religious interest of the Pentateuch culminates in the Book of Deuteronomy. Here, as we read it in the light of historical criticism, the prophetic teaching of the previous century, that of Amos, Isaiah, Micah, and especially Hosea, was gathered up and enshrined. Here we find the great declaration of the oneness of Yahweh (as opposed to the many Baalim) which has been given a central place in Jewish worship as its great confession of monotheism (Deut. vi. 4 ff.). This belief found concrete expression in the centralization of all worship in Jerusalem (Deut. xii). The moral emphasis and humanitarianism of the book is another instance of the prophetic influence, as is the third great feature of it —the doctrine of divine retribution. This last was of special importance for the writing of history in Israel, as we shall see in the subsequent books.

(*e*) Finally, we may notice the conception which underlies that outline of priestly history (P), which is usually regarded as being the literary framework of the Pentateuch as a whole, from the Creation onwards (Gen. i). In this history, the dominant purpose seems to be to write an introduction to the divine law, and to exemplify it. This purpose explains some of the omissions—e.g., those of the building of local altars by the patriarchs, the sacrifice of Isaac, the immorality of the Sodomites and of Lot's daughters, the dispute between Abraham and Lot, the cowardice and lying of Abraham, and the story of Hagar. On the other hand, the positive emphasis falls on the covenants with Noah (Gen. ix), with Abraham (Gen. xvii), and with Israel through Moses (Ex. xxxi. 13), including the instructions given to him for the making of the tabernacle (Ex. xxv-xxxi). As Driver has indicated (*Introduction*, pp. 128 and 129) the culminating promise is that of Ex. xxix. 43-46, which declares "the abiding presence of God with His people Israel . . . symbolized by the 'Tent of Meeting,' surrounded by its immediate attendants, in the centre of the camp."

4. *The four historical books* which follow the Pentateuch in our English Bible—viz., Joshua, Judges, 1 and 2 Samuel, 1 and 2 Kings—also follow it in the Hebrew Bible, where they are classed together as "the Former Prophets." (Ruth, following Judges in the English order, is placed amongst the "Writings" which form the third part of the Hebrew Canon.) The Hebrew name for these four books is probably due to the covenient but quite uncritical Jewish theory which assigned authorship of a book to some prominent personage in it—in this instance Joshua is said to have written his own Book, Samuel the Books of Samuel and Judges, Jeremiah the Books of Kings. The classification of these books together is so far warranted by the fact that there is a unity of purpose and a less obvious unity of sources in these four books. The purpose is evident: it is to continue the history of Israel from the death of Moses to the downfall of Jerusalem and Judah in 585 B.C. Thus in Joshua we read of the conquest of Canaan (i-xii), the division of the territory amongst the tribes (xiii-xxii), and the farewell discourses and death of Joshua (xxiii, xxiv). In Judges, after a brief account of some tribal conquests (i-ii. 5) which form a parallel rather than a sequel to Joshua, we hear of the defence of

Israel from various enemies through the "judges" or rather "deliverers" (ii. 6–xvi); the last five chapters (xvii-xxi) are appended to tell the story of Micah and the migration of the Danites, and that of the Levite's concubine and the conflict of the tribes with one of their own number, Benjamin, which sprang from the incident. In 1 and 2 Samuel, the story of the priest Eli introduces that of Samuel, the great prophet and leader, and his relations with Saul, the first king (1 Sam. i-xv). Then the figures of Saul and David hold the stage, together or apart (1 Sam. xvi-2 Sam. viii), whilst in the third part of the Books we enter on the brilliant narrative known as "the Court History of David" (2 Sam. ix-xx). The last four chapters (xxi-xxiv) again form an appendix to the history of David, and describe events linked to a famine and pestilence, and his wars with the Philistines, and also contain two poems ascribed to him. In 1 and 2 Kings, we begin with a continuation of the "Court History"—the rebellion of Adonijah, and the accession of Solomon (i–ii. 11), and then pass to the reign of Solomon (1 Kings ii. 12–xi), after which, in more summary fashion, we have the parallel history of Israel and Judah until the downfall of Israel in 722 (1 Kings xii–2 Kings xvii), and the history of Judah till its downfall in 586 (2 Kings xviii-xxv).

This evident unity of purpose corresponds with

the unity of sources which linked these books together in their making. In fact, it would be justifiable, apart from convenience, to treat these sources separately, as was done with the Pentateuch. These books (as distinct from their original sources) were composed in their present form to continue the history of the Pentateuch. Such a sequel is anticipated by it (cf. e.g. Num. xxxii. 16 ff.; Deut. i. 3-8; Num. xxvii. 4, representing JE, D, and P respectively). First of all we must "think away" the division of 1 and 2 Samuel, and of 1 and 2 Kings which did not exist in the Hebrew, and was first made by the Septuagint, though in the early Christian centuries Jewish scholars still treated each pair as a unit. Then we find that the sources of Joshua are exactly those of the Pentateuch —viz., J, E, D, and P—so that it has been customary for scholars to treat Joshua with the previous five books, and call the six the "Hexateuch." The work of JE (or of similar writers) continues apparently into Judges and 1 and 2 Samuel, where we have the same kind of duplicate narratives (see p. 61), whilst the editorial work of D is very marked in Judges, slightly present in 1 and 2 Samuel, and again dominant in 1 and 2 Kings, which seems to have been composed (from different sources) to complete the history of the kingdoms down to the time of the editors themselves. Further evidence of unity may be seen from the fact that Judges ii. 6 (after the parallel account of invasion) links directly with Joshua xxiv. 28 ff. most of which it repeats almost verbatim, that 1 Samuel i-xii really continues the story of the "judge" Samuel, and might as well have been part of Judges, and that 1 Kings i, ii belongs to the "Court History" of David, which it continues from 2 Samuel xx. (The appendix, as we shall see, is a manifest interpolation.)

We may now turn to the more detailed study of the four books. In the first, Joshua receives divine encouragement to attempt the task of conquering Canaan, and calls the warriors of tribes already settled east of Jordan (viz., Reuben, Gad, and half-Manasseh) to help their still unsettled brethren. Spies are sent across into Jericho, the Jordan is crossed by a miracle like that of the passage of the Red Sea, the rite of circumcision is performed on the new generation. After Joshua's vision of "the captain of Yahweh's hosts," the walls of Jericho fall by another miracle. But the attempt on Ai is unsuccessful, owing to Achan's theft of spoil "devoted" to Yahweh; he and his family are accordingly stoned and burnt. Ai is then captured by an ambush. At this point there is an intruding section (viii. 30-35), describing a ceremony of blessing and cursing near to Shechem—i.e., in territory as yet unconquered (in fact, no account

55

of the conquest of the centre of the land is given in the book). The previous narrative then goes on to speak of the ruse by which the Gibeonites secured an alliance with Israel, and of the aid given by Israel when they were consequently attacked by the five kings of the south. These are defeated by the aid of a storm of hail, and the five kings put to death. After a summary of other victories in the south (x), the parallel victory over a northern alliance is briefly mentioned (xi), and the first half of the book is rounded off by a list of thirty-one conquered kings (xii). The significant feature is that the conquest is here represented as complete: "Joshua took the whole land, according to all that Yahweh spake unto Moses; and Joshua gave it for an inheritance unto Israel according to their divisions by their tribes" (xi. 23).

This partition is described in the second half of the book (xiii-xxiv), which is largely a geography, corresponding to the history of the first part. Cities of refuge and Levitical cities are appointed in xx and xxi. The last three chapters are an appendix, describing the relations of the western and eastern tribes (xxii), and giving two distinct farewell addresses of Joshua, of which the second (xxiv), delivered at Shechem, links with the intruding passage, viii. 30-35.

The plan of the book is therefore simple and

straightforward, but closer examination shows that elements of different date and authorship underlie this apparent unity. That the book cannot be by Joshua is clear, not only from the fact that it describes his own death, but also from references implying a later age ("unto this day," ix. 27, xv. 63; cf. xix. 47, 48), and especially from the internal contradictions as to the completeness of the conquest (xiii. 13, xv. 14-19, 63, xvi. 10, xvii, 11-13, 14-18, xix. 47). The Israelites, it is said, did not conquer Jerusalem, Gezer, the Plain of Esdraelon, etc., which were the most important parts of Canaan, and some of them were unable to maintain themselves even where they had settled. This evidence is corroborated by that of Judges i-ii. 5, which also shows that the conquest was "by divers portions and divers manners." All our other evidence confirms this, and we may regard such references as belonging to the earliest stratum of the book, usually assigned to J, whereas the Elohistic source (xxiv) represents the conquest as completed by Joshua. In the first half of the book, also, inconsistencies and duplications suggest the continuance of the double tradition of J and E. Thus, in the account of the crossing of the Jordan, Joshua sets up twelve memorial stones twice over—in the bed of the river (iv. 9), and at Gilgal (iv. 20); the people who have crossed the river once in iii. 17 cross it again in iv. 11.

In the composition of the book as a whole, the already combined JE narratives which continued the story of Israel from those of the Pentateuch were selected and edited by a writer of the Deuteronomistic school—i.e., someone writing after 621. This may be seen from a comparison of the opening exhortation to Joshua (i. 3-9) with similar addresses in Deuteronomy. The evidence of this writer's work is chiefly to be found in the first half of Joshua. In the second half the work of priestly writers predominates, though it is not, as in the Pentateuch, the framework, but simply one of the incorporated elements. In x. 12, 13 there is an interesting quotation from "The Book of Jashar," a source now lost, but earlier than JE.

The Book of Judges has three clearly marked divisions. The first part (i. 1–ii. 5) was prefixed by a later editor, as being an early and independent account of parts of the conquest (see above); as it stands, it interrupts the continuous story from Joshua xxiv. 28 ff., which is resumed (with an overlap) in what is now the second part of the book, ii. 6-xvi. This names twelve (or if we include Abimelech, thirteen) hero-leaders of Israel before the monarchy, but nothing is recorded of six of them, whilst Othniel, one of the other six (iii. 9-11), is little more than mentioned. We are left with five, excluding Abimelech—viz., Ehud who assassinates Eglon of Moab, Deborah (with Barak) who leads against Sisera in the north, Gideon against the Midianites (Arab nomads), Jephthah against the Ammonites (east of Reuben and south of Jabbok), and Samson against the Philistines. The story of Abimelech, the son of Gideon by a Shechemite concubine (viii. 31, ix), stands apart from the rest, and suggests an early attempt at kingship with Canaanite support.

The stories of these "heroes" carry us back to the early days of Israel in Canaan, and the kind of life they represent has little enough to do with the organized religion of later times, in spite of the inclusion of "Gideon, Barak, Samson, Jephthah" amongst the heroes of faith enumerated in the Epistle to the Hebrews, and their partial canonization in the Book of Judges itself. We now read these primitive stories in a Deuteronomistic framework (e.g., iii. 12-15, 29, 30, the setting of the original story given in vv. 16-28). Its theory of divine retribution in national history is clearly stated in ii. 11-23; there was a constantly repeated cycle of Baalism, divine wrath, foreign oppression, appeal to Yahweh, divine help through one of these deliverers, relapse into Baalism after his death. Another anachronistic element also comes from the editorial setting. Each deliverer is represented as ruling over a united Israel, which did not exist at this time, and only for a generation or two later. The stories show that these heroes were local, not national figures, and some of them may have been contemporaneous, so that the chronology, with its total of 410 years, deserves no credence.

The third division of the book (xvii-xxi) is an appendix, standing outside the editorial scheme. This has preserved for us the remarkable story of Micah and the Danites, which throws so much light on early conditions of life and religion in Israel (xvii, xviii), and the not less remarkable story of the Levite and his concubine—a piece of grim but impressive realism— leading to the account of the vengeance taken on Benjamin and its sequel (xix-xxi). The stories, apart from editorial (priestly) expansions of the latter, are early.

Thus, the Book of Judges consists of early material (the earliest being the Song of Deborah, *c.* 1100 B.C.) which has been taken over to form its central part by a Deuteronomistic editor (*c.* 600); the first part and the third were added (*c.* 400) by a priestly writer, again using much earlier material.

The section of the continuous history now called 1 and 2 Samuel is divided by summaries into three main parts, and as in previous sections there is an appendix. The first summary (1, xiv. 47-52) gives Saul's victories and relatives, and concludes his life prior to his rejection and (gradual) replacement by David. The second (2, viii) describes David's campaigns at greater length, and adds a list of his chief officers. The third (2, xx. 23-26) repeats this list at the end of the account of Absalom's rebellion.

In the first division, continuing the main part of Judges, the story of Eli not only introduces Samuel from his birth, but also explains the disasters which befell Eli and his family and the ark of which they were guardians. The destruction of the Shiloh temple is not stated, though it must have come into the original narrative; it has been replaced by an impossible story of a complete victory over the Philistines won by Samuel—impossible, because all the subsequent narrative shows that the Philistines were *not* subdued as stated in vii. 13. In cc. viii-xii there is yet clearer evidence of composite authorship, in the double tradition of the election of Saul. In the narrative of ix. 1–x. 16, xi. 1-11, 15, Saul goes out to seek his father's asses, and comes across the seer or prophet Samuel, who anoints him secretly for the kingship, the choice being confirmed by the spirit of ecstatic prophesying which comes on Saul; Samuel is acting voluntarily, according to divine instructions. After a month, Saul seizes the opportunity of an Ammonite outrage to rouse Israel, and is eventually made king in Gilgal. In the narrative of viii. 1-22, x. 17-24, xii, which seems to continue the story of Samuel in vii, Samuel is a "judge," but when in his old age his sons act for him the people are dissatisfied with their conduct and ask for a king. This demand arouses the displeasure of both Samuel and Yahweh, and Samuel warns them of what a king will do in terms that show considerable experience of life under an Oriental monarch. However, the people are gathered to Mizpah, where Saul is elected king by the operation of the sacred lot. Saul's closing address (xii) rounds off the period of the "judges," much as Joshua's (Joshua xxiv) rounded off that of the conquest. The second narrative is obviously later in character, and its disapproval of the kingship corresponds with that of Hosea (xiii. 11). This may be the continued narrative of E, as the other may be that of J, which probably represents the true manner of development from tribal groups to some sort of national unity under a king. The remaining two chapters (xiii, xiv) of this division continue this earlier narrative, and describe the success of Saul and Jonathan against the Philistines at Michmash.

The second division (1, xv–2, vii) begins with one of the two stories of the rejection of Saul, that of the sparing of Agag and the Amalekite spoil (for the other see xiii. 7-15). This is followed by a double tradition of David's emergence. In the earlier (xvi.

14-23, xviii. 6-14, 20-29, xix. 11-17), David is the harpist summoned to charm away Saul's madness, who becomes his armour-bearer; Saul jealous of his growing fame as a warrior plots against him; Michal, the daughter of Saul whom David has married, helps him to escape. In the later (xvii–xviii. 5, 17-19, xix. 1-10), David the shepherd-lad comes up to the camp to see his brothers, and first wins the notice of Saul by slaying Goliath. As in the other story, Saul plots against David, now married to another daughter of Saul, Merab; the spear flung at David by Saul misses him, and he escapes. Some of the incidents of David's wanderings as an outlaw also appear to be doublets, such as the two similar accounts of Saul's life being spared by David (xxiv and xxvi). In the last five chapters of the first Book (xxvii-xxxi) we see David taking refuge amongst Israel's enemies, the Philistines, and the events leading to the death of Saul and Jonathan on Gilboa (the story of the "witch of Endor," xxviii. 3-25, should come after xxx, and on the eve of the battle; the geography confirms this). In the second Book, the "Lament" of David over Saul and Jonathan is followed by the account of his kingship over Judah in Hebron, its extension to all Israel, and the removal of his capital to the now conquered Jerusalem. This division culminates in the removal of the ark to Jerusalem, and the promise of "an everlasting throne" to David.

The third division (2, ix-xx) consists of the great literary treasure of this section, the "Court History of David," of which more will be said later. It is now divided from the first two chapters of 1 Kings, which originally belonged to it, by the appendix to David's history (successive insertions made here as the last opportunity before the events leading to the accession of Solomon). This appendix is critically interesting and suggestive of the gradual accretions of literary material. There are two similar events, a famine sent to punish Saul's slaughter of the Gibeonites, and the expiation of this slaughter by the execution of seven descendants of Saul, on the one hand (xxi. 1-14), and on the other, the pestilence sent because of David's census of the people (xxiv. 1-25). Within this opening and closing material, once doubtless continuous, there has been inserted again an account of David's wars with the Philistines, and a list of his "mighty men" (xxi. 15-22 and xxiii. 8-39). But once more this has been divided by another insertion, that of two poems ascribed to David—viz., the 18th Psalm and his "Last Words" (xxii and xxiii. 1-7).

The earliest document in 1 and 2 Samuel is the almost contemporary "Court History of David," followed not long after by an account of the rise of the monarchy. At a later date (perhaps about 700 B.C.) there was added the different story which views the monarchy unfavourably. Later still, perhaps about 600, these stories and the "Court History" were combined by the Deuteronomistic editors, though they seem to have added comparatively little of their own.

It is far otherwise with 1 and 2 Kings, of which the general framework for the post-Solomonic reigns has been supplied by the Deuteronomists, much as in the Book of Judges. In any case, a different scale of treatment was necessary, for "Kings" covers four centuries (970-586) whilst "Samuel" covers one only, and tradition and record had doubtless been much fuller for David and Solomon than for their less distinguished successors, so that there was less material extant by the time of the exile. There are three principal divisions, the first dealing with Solomon (1, i-xi), the second with the northern and southern kingdoms in parallelism (1, xii-2, xvii), and the third with the surviving southern kingdom after the fall of Samaria in 722 (2, xviii-xxv). As we have seen, the first two chapters belong to the "Court History" of the previous book, and describe the last days of David and the accession of Solomon. The rest of the first division centres in the great buildings of Solomon which are described in vi and vii. Around this point, of primary interest to a later generation, there have been gathered narratives illustrating the piety and sagacity of Solomon (iii), his administration of the kingdom and wide knowledge (iv), his agreement with Hiram of Tyre for building materials, and his levy of workers from all Israel (v and ix), the bringing of the ark into the new temple, and its dedication (viii), the visit of the Queen of Sheba and Solomon's wealth (x), his numerous marriages, recognition of foreign religions, and adversaries (xi).

In the second part of the work, covering about two centuries, the distinctive feature is supplied by the formulæ and method of the compiler. He has to keep the annals of the two kingdoms which emerged after Solomon moving together, and, short of using parallel columns, he has adopted the best possible device. His method is to synchronize the beginning of the reign of one of the two contemporary kings with the particular year of the other king's reign, to complete his account of the first, and then to go back and pick up the thread of the parallel record. He also gives us the accession-age of the king, the length of his reign, the name of the queen-mother (an important personage), and a verdict (from the Deuteronomistic standpoint) on the king's character. This is the formula for the kings of Judah; that for Israel is somewhat briefer (cf. e.g. 1 Kings xv. 9-11, 23, 24, the intervening verses being the material derived from the sources).

These sources are frequently mentioned by name. Thus we hear once of "The Book of the Acts of Solomon" (1 Kings xi. 41), seventeen times of "The Book of the Chronicles of the Kings of Israel," and fifteen times of "The Book of the Chronicles of the Kings of Judah." Nothing is known of these sources, save what we may infer from the material given in "Kings." There are also other sources, not mentioned by name, but evidently used, such as collections of stories about the prophets, especially relating to the northern kingdom, temple records, naturally referring to the southern kingdom, and a biography of Isaiah (2 Kings xviii. 17-xx. 19), which seems to have been taken (like Isaiah xxxvi-xxxix) from some earlier source (thus twice reproduced). In the third part of the book, relating to Judah alone after 722, the synchronisms with the north are, of course, wanting. The compiler's own contribution naturally increases as we approach his own times, which we may put somewhere about 600.

We have now before us, in the Pentateuch and the "Former Prophets," the only consecutive outline of the history of Israel which the Old Testament affords; the Chronicler will give us an "ecclesiastical" edition of it, and some of the sources he includes will illuminate the foundation of Judaism in post-exilic times, whilst the First Book of Maccabees will tell of a temporary revival of political nationalism. But this is the proper place to ask what impression the history of Israel in its period of political freedom ought to make upon us, when we read the consecutive story observantly and critically.

We have seen, in the "Former Prophets," that the idealized conquest of Canaan, representing it as achieved completely from the outset, was historically untrue and that the "conquest" was gradual; or rather, as the history of the separate tribes shows, it was a process of absorption and peaceful penetration, through which Israel overcame the Canaanites, politically and nationally. Politically and nationally—but not religiously, so far as the rank and file of Israel was concerned. Here the conquered was the conqueror, and the religion of the desert was baptized into Baalism in becoming the religion of Israel in Canaan. Against this the great prophets whom we have yet to study made their minority protest, and we may broadly describe that protest as the survival of the nomadic religion, with a new application of its social morality and a new extension of the realms of Yahweh. Nevertheless, even before the great prophets, it was the religion of Yahweh that was the nucleus of tribal unity and the promise of national unity. In

the Song of Deborah, the greatest piece of literature
in the earliest period, we see both the struggle with
the Canaanites that disproves the ideal of a complete
conquest, and the gathering of certain of the northern
tribes in the name of Yahweh to repel the common
danger. Again, it was the danger from without
which gave the impetus to more organized union in
the days of Samuel. The Philistines seemed to be
masters of Canaan; it was prophetic "enthusiasm" (in
the etymological sense) which found expression both
in the kingmaker and the first king himself, and began
the struggle which David was to carry to a successful
issue. The character of David, in the narratives of
his early life and especially in the "Court History," is
one of the most interesting features of the literature
before us; the latter narrative is full of graphic and
convincing detail, written in the best style of classical
Hebrew. There is no moralizing, but a grim sense
of the Hebrew equivalent for "Nemesis" hangs over
the story of David's adultery with Bathsheba, the
rape of Tamar by her half-brother Amnon, the
murder of Amnon by her full brother Absalom, the
exile of Absalom and eventually his rebellion, the
frustrated attempt of Adonijah to secure his inheritance, and the final picture of the senile king, the mere
tool of court intrigue, and meditating a posthumous
vengeance which he dare not execute. How much

better to die with Saul on Gilboa, than on such a deathbed of helpless decay!

The place given to Solomon in our literature is justified both by the importance of the temple he built and by the consequences of his tyranny and extortion in the division of a kingdom never really welded into one. After him the most striking figure is Ahab, the political importance of his reign being obscured by the fact that he seems to the reader little more than a foil for the fiery patriotism of Elijah. Perhaps the next most striking incident on which the eye of the reader lingers is the rebellion and successful revolution of Jehu, so vividly and dramatically told. In this period the nearer background is Aramaea and the farther is Assyria; it is the latter which becomes dominant in the following century, the eighth, and leads to the emergence of the interpreting prophets. Amongst them, the most prominent is Isaiah, whose career epitomizes the history of half a century in the public affairs of Judah. Next to him in historical importance comes Jeremiah in the closing decades of the following century, whose work extends from before the reformation to Josiah on to the downfall of the city.

In this literature, the more impressively because through example rather than precept, the lesson of all history is exhibited with peculiar emphasis—the dominance of the spiritual factors over the physical, the power of the attitude of human personality over the events which seem to crush it, yet are forced at last to yield to its own interpretation of them. This is seen most of all in Jeremiah, in whom the religion of the older Israel reaches its highest point, and the foundation of a new and more individualizing religion is laid.

5. The third division of the historical writings of the Old Testament is the work of the "Chronicler," by which term we designate the writer or writers to whom are due the four books, 1 and 2 Chronicles, Ezra, and Nehemiah. This is the chronological order, and is preserved in the English Bible; in the Hebrew Bible, however, the order is Ezra-Nehemiah (one book), 1 and 2 Chronicles, and these are the closing books of the Canon—i.e., they are grouped with the "Writings," its third division. The reason for the reversed order is probably that Ezra-Nehemiah, as presenting new and important material, was first added, whilst Chronicles was omitted as simply a new edition (as indeed it is) of the earlier historical books; later on, but now out of order, it was added as worthy of remembrance. Originally Chronicles-Ezra-Nehemiah was a unity of compilation, as is clearly shown by a study of the language and general characteristics of the books. Its object was to write a

continuous history of *Judah* from the beginning of
the world down to the establishment of Judaism
through Ezra and Nehemiah. The first nine chapters
of 1 Chronicles link Saul with Adam by means of
genealogical tables. Saul is dismissed in a single chapter (x) and the history proper begins with David
and his capture of Jerusalem (xi). We hear of his
captains and his armies (xi, xii), the removal of the
ark to the house of Obed-edom (xiii), the overthrow
of the Philistines (xiv), the further removal of the
ark to Jerusalem (xv, xvi), David's desire to build
the temple (xvii), his victories (xviii-xx), the census and pestilence which led to the choice of a site for
the temple (xxi) and David's preparations for the
building of the temple and its ministry, to which no
less than eight chapters are allotted (xxii-xxix). The
first nine chapters of 2 Chronicles belong to Solomon and his accomplishment of this task; we hear of
his wealth and his agreement with Hiram (i, ii), the
actual work of building (iii, iv), the dedication of
the building (v-vii), Solomon's general administration (viii), and the visit of the Queen of Sheba (ix).
With the tenth chapter we pass to Rehoboam and the
kings of Judah, whilst the kings of Israel are ignored
so far as is possible, the history of Judah being traced
down to 586. Throughout, the text of 1 and 2 Kings
is followed verbatim, except for important and char-

acteristic omissions and expansions. Thus David's domestic history, with all its discreditable incidents, is passed over in silence, as are Solomon's foreign wives, idolatry, and adversaries (cf. 1 Kings xi); on the other hand, the four verses in 2 Kings xviii. 3-6 which describe the reformation of Hezekiah are expanded by the Chronicler into four chapters (2, xxix-xxxii). The closing paragraph of 2 Chronicles is identical with the opening verses of Ezra (i. 1-3*a*), and records the decree of Cyrus permitting the Jews to return to Jerusalem. Probably it was copied from Ezra to make a "happy ending" to Chronicles and indeed to the Canon.

The Book of Ezra ought to perplex the careful reader. After quoting the decree of Cyrus, it goes on to describe the response to it of the Jews under *Sheshbazzar*, and the material support they received from Cyrus (i). There follows a list of groups alleged to have returned, in which the name of *Zerubbabel* replaces that of Sheshbazzar (ii. 2). In the seventh month (presumably of the same year, 537) the people are at Jerusalem (iii. 1), where, under the leadership of Joshua and Zerubbabel, they *erect the altar* and keep the Feast of Tabernacles. In the second year they lay *the foundation of the temple* (iii. 10). But people of the old northern kingdom, to whom co-operation in this work is denied, calumniate them at the Persian court, with the result that the temple-building is checked until the reign of Darius —i.e., 521 (iv. 5). The following section (iv. 6-23) says that accusation was made in the beginning of the reign of Ahasuerus—i.e., Xerxes (485-465)— and that in the days of his successor Artaxerxes (464-425), certain named persons wrote accusing the Jews of building, not the temple, but the city and its walls, with a view to rebellion (iv. 12, 13). This document is given in Aramaic, which extends beyond it (iv. 8– vi. 18) into the subsequent narrative. In the Aramaic document, Artaxerxes replies forbidding the work, which ceases until the time of—Darius! i.e., *the previous reign but one* (iv. 24). Of course, it is evident what has happened. The document related to events about the middle of the fifth century, perhaps seventy years after the beginning of the reign of Darius, possibly the events which stirred Nehemiah to action. It has been misunderstood by the editors of the book, who have used it in the wrong place. In ch. v we return therefore to the suspended work of the building of the temple. In 521, Haggai and Zechariah stir the Jews to a new effort, against which Tattenai, the governor of Syria, raises a new objection, which is referred to Darius. He however permits and supports the work, and the temple is finished in 516-515 (March). The Passover is celebrated, and in ch.

vii, the phrase "after these things" covers a gap of at least 57 and possibly 118 years—viz., from 515 to 458 or 397. In this seventh year of Artaxerxes, Ezra returns to Jerusalem by royal permission (letter of Artaxerxes, vii. 12-26, in Aramaic). On arrival he hears of the Jewish marriages to foreign women, and confesses the sin of the people in a long prayer. The people are moved to put away their foreign wives, and a list of culprits is given.

The Book of Nehemiah begins independently with an autobiographical narrative, describing the sorrow of the cupbearer of Artaxerxes on hearing of the distressful and defenceless condition of Jerusalem (444). The king appoints him to go and build the city; he succeeds in building up the wall, in spite of the opposition and threats of neighbours, and the economic distress. He puts his brother and the governor of the castle in charge of Jerusalem. In ch. vii occurs the same list of returned exiles as was found in Ezra ii.

In all this there has been no mention of Ezra, who suddenly appears in ch. viii as reading from the book of the Law to a great assembly, which pledges itself to obedience and keeps the Feast of Tabernacles, followed by a day of fasting and confession (ix) and a solemn covenant (ix. 38) of which the terms are given in ch. x. In Nehemiah xi, Ezra disappears as suddenly as he appeared, and we resume the narrative of Nehemiah exactly at the point at which it was interrupted by the list (vii. 4)—viz., the difficulty caused by the scantiness of the population of Jerusalem. This is now met by volunteer settlers and others chosen by lot, and lists are given, after which the wall is dedicated (xii. 27 ff.). In xiii. 6, we hear that Nehemiah, who had apparently been absent from Jerusalem for twelve years, returned to find certain abuses which needed attention, such as the misuse of temple buildings by foreigners, neglect to raise proper provision for Levites, the profanation of the Sabbath, and marriages with foreign women, which are henceforth forbidden.

It is plain that there are a number of historical problems here which cannot be discussed within our present scope. But two things may be said summarily—that Nehemiah viii-x probably belongs to the "Memoirs" of Ezra, and that the double mention of Nehemiah in it (viii. 9, x. 1) may be due to the compiler who incorporated this portion in our present "Nehemiah," and that it is also probable that Ezra came to Jerusalem "in the seventh year" of the second Artaxerxes, not the first—i.e., in 397. In a number of ways this would make a better historical sequence.

The sources used by the Chronicler were pri-

marily the canonical books of "Samuel" and "Kings,"
a "Midrash" (R.V. "Commentary") of "the book of
the kings" (2 Chron. xxiv. 27), which was an expanded form of the canonical "Kings," and may have
been the form in which the Chronicler used it, some
similar work giving stories of prophets, the "Memoirs" of Nehemiah and Ezra, which are data of first-
class importance, and certain Aramaic documents of
varying quality. We can study his use of some of
his material by a comparison of, say, the bringing up
of the ark to Jerusalem as told in 2 Samuel vi. 12 ff.
with the account in 1 Chronicles xv, xvi, in which
everything is done according to the ideas of one who
believed that the Priestly Law actually observed by
his contemporaries of say 300-250 B.C. had been similarly observed from the earliest days, especially by
so devout an ecclesiastic as David. The Chronicler
brings down his genealogies to the sixth generation
after Zerubbabel, say to about 350, and he mentions Jaddua (Neh. xii. 11, 22) who belongs to the
time of Alexander. The Persian Empire already lies
for him in the past, or he would not have found it
necessary to say that Cyrus was "the king of Persia."
The historical value of his additions to "Samuel"
and "Kings" may not be great, but his work is nevertheless of much importance as evidence of the priestly, or rather of the Levitical, interest in religious rites

and institutions. Also we must be grateful to him for having preserved the genuine documents that illuminate the period of Nehemiah and Ezra.

6. Only brief mention can be made of three books which are most conveniently classed here, not because they are "history," but because they have narrative form—viz., Ruth, Jonah, and Esther. Two of them—viz., Ruth and Esther—belong to the five "Megilloth" or "rolls" which are read at notable seasons of the Jewish calendar—Ruth at Pentecost and Esther at Purim (March). The Book of Ruth is a graceful story of a woman of Moab, the widow of a Hebrew emigrant to Moab, who returns with her mother-in-law, Naomi, to the native country of the family and its home, Bethlehem. Here is discovered a kinsman, Boaz, who marries Ruth. Their son, Obed, is destined to be the father of Jesse and the grandfather of king David. The story is told with much real art, and with evident delight in the story for its own sake. There is also interest in the ancient custom of the transfer of legal right by symbolic act. The story shows genuine faith in the guiding hand of God. But the repeated emphasis on "Ruth the Moabitess" points to something more—the presence of a foreigner in the royal lineage, and this foreigner one of a hated nation (Deut. xxiii. 3). This is an implicit challenge to the policy, dating from

Nehemiah and Ezra, which sought to suppress such marriages. Thus the book would seem to echo the broader outlook of Deutero-Isaiah, and its keynote would be the blessing of Boaz on "Ruth the Moabitess" (ii. 12).

The Book of Jonah is formally classed amongst the "Latter Prophets" of the Hebrew Canon, but it is really a didactic story of a disobedient prophet whose narrow nationalism earned divine rebuke. Nothing is known of the prophet whose name is borrowed for the story (2 Kings xiv. 25), or why it was so borrowed. It belongs to the same general period as "Ruth," and has similar aims. The reference to Nineveh as a city of the past, and the character of the language, point to a later rather than an earlier date in the post-exilic period. Its sympathy with both children and animals (iv. 11) should be noted. The psalm of thanksgiving has been subsequently inserted into the story, and was not composed for it. As has often been said, it is one of the tragedies of literature and religion that a story with so much of the Christian gospel in it should be chiefly known to the world as a story about a fish and made either matter of ridicule, or what is even worse, a test of orthodoxy.

At the other extreme to the true catholicity of Ruth and Jonah is the Book of Esther, the most un-

Christian of Old Testament books. It is the highly dramatic account of a deliverance of Jews from their enemies in the time of Ahasuerus (Xerxes, 485-465). The king, offended by his queen, Vashti, decides to replace her, and after four years, fixes on Esther, who is, unknown to him, a Jewess. Her cousin, Mordecai, gives offence to Haman, the prime minister, who thereupon secures a royal edict to exterminate the Jews. Esther intervenes, having been prompted by her cousin, who had previously rendered a great though forgotten service to the king. The result is that Haman is hanged on the gallows he had built for Mordecai, who replaces him, and the Jews are allowed to kill 75,800 of their enemies. Hence, the Jews have since kept the festival of Purim.

Like the apocryphal Book of Judith, the story is full of improbabilities or impossibilities. The queen of Xerxes at this time was Amestris, not Esther. Mordecai is said to have been carried captive from Jerusalem in 597 (ii. 6), which would make him at least 120 years old when he began his political career as prime minister. The conduct of a Persian king in allowing the Jews to kill so many thousands of his subjects is incredible. The book, in fact, is not religious at all (it makes no mention of God), but is an exaltation of nationalism at its worst, and falls below the level of the *lex talionis* which Jesus condemned.

Esther herself, after the Jews in Shushan have killed 500, asks for another day of killing, which accounts for 300 more, and she has the ten sons of Haman hanged. We may be glad to think that such a story is an unhistorical romance intended to account for an existent festival of Purim (cf. 2 Macc. xv. 36), and probably written after the Maccabean Rebellion. It is possible that the festival itself was of Babylonian origin, and that the Babylonian Jews had become so accustomed to it that they needed some explanation of their own practice. In that case, a pagan origin for the festival would be fitly matched by a pagan story about it, whose one gleam of light is the appeal of Mordecai to Esther to sacrifice herself for her people's sake, and her loyal response to it (iv. 14-16).

CHAPTER IV

PROPHECY AND APOCALYPTIC

1. Our survey of the writing of Old Testament history has already shown the shaping influence of prophetic teaching upon it. History is the interpretation of events seen in their proper sequence and relation. But the human consciousness, even in the first observer of an event, cannot take cognizance of it without in some degree interpreting it; there are no "bare" facts for the historian. The observer's inevitable interpretation of the event may become, in turn, a new "fact" of history. The primacy of the Hebrew prophets in the religion of Israel is due to their creation of historic "facts" by their interpretations of events, to say nothing of their frequent political role in the making of those events. From their interpretation and the teaching based upon it flowed not only the principles on which the history of Israel came to be written, but also the final presentation of the devotional, ethical, and legal literature which meets us as Psalms, Wisdom, and the Law.

Prophecy was essentially a message of God to the prophet's contemporaries. As such it was naturally and ordinarily spoken and not written, and

82

we have already seen (Ch. II) its oral beginnings. Only when the message failed to gain attention did the prophets turn to making a written record (as we may see explicitly in Isa. viii. 16, xxx. 8; Jer. xxxvi), as a testimony to another generation. The conditions of Hebrew prophecy were fourfold—viz., the general setting of Hebrew psychology, the vocational experience of the prophets as distinct from other men, the "corporate personality" which identified them with both God and Israel, and the background of creative and interpreted history.

(*a*) Hebrew psychology has three primary characteristics. (1) Life and all the phenomena of consciousness were ascribed to a principle identified with the breath. (2) Psychical functions were ascribed not to the brain and the nervous system, but to the body in general, both to its central and to its peripheral organs—heart, kidneys, bowels, eye, ear, tongue, hand, and even the flesh and bones in a sort of diffused consciousness. (3) Anything strange or abnormal in human character and conduct could be explained as due to "possession" by an invasive "spirit." We must not read the Old Testament with the spectacles of Greek dualism; for the Hebrew, man is an animated body, not an incarnated soul. According to Genesis ii. 7, God made man (completely) of clay, and then "animated" the figure by living breath blown into his nostrils, so that he became a living being. Exactly the same thing occurs in Ezekiel's valley of dry bones (xxxvii), where the men are first reformed, and then comes the animating spirit-wind to fill their bodies and give them life. Such life, dependent on God from the beginning, could always be increased or deceased at His will.

(*b*) The peculiar and vocational experience of the prophets was such an increase of this "life" that their organs became, for the time being, the very organs of God. They felt the beating of God's heart as their own; their eyes became the eyes of God seeing things unseen by men; their ears rang with the cry of human rebellion as though they were His. All this was no figure of speech to them, but sheer stark reality, and it is no wonder that their conduct was often abnormal and strange, even to their fellow-countrymen, so strange that they could be called "madmen." Without such abnormal or "ecstatic" phenomena, it is doubtful whether any man would have felt his call to be a prophet, or would have been received as a prophet by others.

(*c*) Thus "possessed" by God, and admitted into His heavenly council, the prophet could be conscious of uniting Israel to God and God to Israel. The prophet's own relation to his people is expressed through the ancient category of "corporate personality." This is a conception strange to the modern mind, for our sense of "social solidarity" is of a different order, denoting as it does the combination of individuals on the basis of common interest or obligation. "Corporate personality," on the other hand, denotes the primitive idea of a family, a clan, a tribe, or a nation as one, so that on occasion the whole group and the individual member of it may be treated as identical, whether in law or religion, with fluidity of transition from the one to the many and *vice versa*. Thus the prophet can feel, not only that he represents, but that he actually *is* Israel. How deep a pathos this consciousness adds, both to intercession and to exhortation, is easily apparent, as is also its relation to the social morality of the corporate personality which he demands in the name of the God of Israel.

(*d*) Finally, there is, in the creative centuries of Hebrew history, the background of historic events which the prophet interprets. Prophecy never lived and throve in a vacuum; it had to have something to interpret. It found God, but it found Him in the course of actual events; it was stirred to utterance by them, and was never born of isolation and detachment from them. The great events which matter most (after the Exodus) are those that sprang from Israel's relation to the two empires, first of Assyria and then of Babylonia. In the ninth century, Ahab fought against Assyria at Karkar, and Jehu paid tribute, but it was not until the times of Tiglath-Pileser III (745-727) that Assyria directly concerned herself with Israel. In 738 Menahem of Israel paid tribute to him, but in 734 we find Pekah of Israel and Rezon of Damascus in alliance against Assyria, and vainly trying to force Ahaz of Judah to join them— the so-called Syro-Ephraimitic War. The result was the capture of Damascus by Assyria in 732, and the loss of the northern part of Israel's territory. In 727, Hoshea of Israel, in confederacy with Egypt, refused the customary tax, which led to the fall of Samaria in 722. In the closing years of the century, Sennacherib (704-682) marched against revolting states in Syria, amongst which was Judah under Hezekiah. Isaiah was vindicated by the deliverance of Jerusalem. Under Manasseh, Judah was a vassal state of Assyria, and there was a great revival of cults other than the Yahwism of the prophets. But about 630, the invasion of the Scythians seems to have stirred Jeremiah to prophecy, as the fall of Nineveh in 612 did Nahum. In 605 the Babylonians succeeded to the place of Assyria, their power lasting only till 538, when it was overthrown by Cyrus. Short as was that period, it was of the greatest political and religious importance. The revolt of Jehoiakim led to the deportation of 597, and that of Zedekiah to the second deportation of 586, transferring the real centre of Judah's life to Babylon. From Babylon came the ultimate movement to rebuild the temple and establish Judaism. But the prophets of the Persian period are all men of secondary rank and importance as compared with the great prophets of the creative centuries.

2. *The Record of Prophecy.* All the work of these men that has come down to us has been for the sake of convenience gathered into four rolls or collections of prophecies, which have been classed under the headings respectively of Isaiah, Jeremiah, Ezekiel, the Twelve. It is instructive to regard the last of the four as an indication of the way in which "Isaiah" has come into being. The Twelve are what we know as the Minor Prophets. They have been incorporated continuously, though the names assigned to the sections have served to distinguish each of these sections from one another. They most of them have received additions to the original nucleus—e.g., Amos ix. 8*b* ff., Zechariah ix ff., which, however, have not been distinguished as such. In regard also to the first roll, that of "Isaiah," the added sections have not been indicated by the names of their authors, so that the whole of the prophetic collections on that roll come to be assigned to Isaiah of Jerusalem. In reading it, criticism must work back from its present state with-

out any prejudice in favour of Isaianic authorship. We have rather to ask how much of the contents of the roll can reasonably be assigned to the Isaiah of Jerusalem who prophesied in the latter half of the eighth century. This is an important principle of criticism which holds just as much for the Psalms, the Wisdom literature, and the Law as for the Prophets. We are not endeavouring to deny to an author this or that passage in a work originally ascribed to him. We are trying to select from a late collection of more or less anonymous prophecy that which formed the original nucleus.

What has been said suggests the chief source of difficulty felt in reading the Prophets—namely, the internal discontinuity. This applies not only to the larger sections of which we have spoken, but also to the paragraphs of the Revised Version. For the most part these smaller sections represent detached oracles which have subsequently been gathered and arranged on what might seem to us quite inadequate grounds of connexion. For example, in the first chapter of Isaiah, verse 9 refers to Sodom and Gomorrah, as also does verse 10. The identity of names has led to the association of the two paragraphs, yet, as a matter of fact, they have different subjects and different occasions. In addition to these detached expressions of prophetic inspiration (see Ch. II), these prophetic books contain autobiographical passages written in the first person and narrative passages written in the third, the latter being probably the work of the prophets' disciples. It will be most convenient for us to study the prophets in their chronological order, especially as this allows us without any violence to combine with it a topical grouping which illustrates the inner logic and development of great truths. Thus we can combine three of the prophets of the eighth century—namely, Amos, Hosea, and Micah—as emphasizing in their different ways the vital connexion of morality and religion. The fourth and greatest prophet of that century, namely Isaiah, might equally well come under this head, but he deserves separate treatment, not only because of his great historical importance, but also because of his emphasis on the "holiness" of Yahweh. We may therefore take him as the prophet of divine transcendence. Our next group of prophets, after the prophetic interregnum under Manasseh, is formed by Zephaniah, Nahum, and Habakkuk, all of them prophets of "the day of the Lord," in their several ways. They may be called prophets of transition, and the next step forward is taken by their younger contemporary Jeremiah, whose name stands for the essential step forward from corporate personality into religious, but still corporate individualism.

This was made more explicit by the next great prophet, Ezekiel, who also made a contribution of his own to future religion, which we may fairly characterize as sacramentalism. The final stage of the great creative movement extending from the eighth to the sixth centuries was that reached by Deutero-Isaiah, in whom the new element may be called evangelism—i.e., the glad news of Israel's own redemption and world mission as the prophet of Yahweh. After this we have, indeed, a number of prophets of the Persian and even the Greek period, but the age may be regarded as that of the decline and fall of prophecy before its completed transition into literary apocalyptic.

3. *The Course of Prophecy.* (*a*) *Morality and Religion.*—Amos was the first of the prophets of whose utterances we have a written record. In vii. 10-17 he denies that he is a professional prophet and says that nothing but divine choice and compulsion have compelled a Judaean farmer to come forward with the message of Yahweh to Judah's greater northern kinsman, Israel. The Book of Amos is formally more systematic and straightforward in its arrangement than most of the prophets. The introduction (i. 1–ii. 5) gives a panoramic view of the sins of Damascus (i. 3-5), Philistia (6-8), Phœnicia (9, 10), Edom (11, 12), Ammon (13-15), Moab (ii. 1-3),

Judah (ii. 4-5), all preparatory to the culminating attack of ii. 6 ff. on the sins of Israel. These are essentially social injustice and immorality, and they are aggravated by the fact that Yahweh had displaced the Amorites for Israel and had sent His messengers to His people, without result. Hence the coming day of judgment when they will be overthrown in battle. This is followed by three addresses (iii. 1-15, iv. 1-13, v. 1–vi. 14) developing the general theme, and five visions of judgment symbolized through locusts (vii. 1-3), fire (4-6), plumbline (7-9), summer fruit (viii. 1-3), the smitten sanctuary (ix. 1-8a). The fourth address (viii. 4-14) has been inserted after the fourth vision, perhaps because the liturgy of Deuteronomy xxvi with its basket of fruit suggested the thanksgiving that Amos saw transformed into mourning. The closing promise of restoration and prosperity (ix. 8b ff.) is of manifestly later date, and illustrates the natural desire to end a book with a promise rather than a threat. But for Amos the day of Yahweh will be His intervention for the sake not of Israel but of righteousness. He prophesied in the prosperous days of Jeroboam II, probably between 760 and 750.

Unlike Amos, Hosea, who prophesied somewhat later, belonged to the northern kingdom. His story is of deep personal interest; his love for his faithless wife (i-iii) revealed to him Yahweh's love for faithless Israel, and he penetrated more deeply than Amos into the idea of religion as a right relation to God. Not less, however, than Amos he urges right conduct towards other men as essential to the true knowledge of Yahweh (iv. 1-6, vi. 6 ff.). He especially denounces the Canaanite influence on the worship of Yahweh and the resulting immorality (iv. 12 ff.). Besides the figure of marriage worked out in ch. ii, Hosea uses that of fatherhood (xi. 1 ff.). It is practically impossible to find any logical order in the body of the book (iv-xiv), which is really a collection of short and passionate utterances against Israel and its rulers, especially the priests. Yet in Hosea, and much more explicitly than in Amos, this denunciation aimed at securing penitence—not the shallow penitence of vi. 1-3, but the true and deep penitence of xiv, which forms a beautiful close to a book of fine humanity and deep religion. The human interest centres in the exegesis of i and iii. It has been keenly discussed whether iii is (*a*) the sequel, (*b*) the parallel, or (*c*) the prelude to i. The view here taken is the conventional one—viz., the first— so that iii, though in the first person, unlike i, really describes Hosea's attempt to win back and restore his faithless wife, who may have been a "sacred" prostitute at one of the sanctuaries. If so, it would

account for the marked bitterness of Hosea against the priests of his day. It is certainly natural to suppose that the evangelical insight of xiv rests on an actual and parallel personal experience described in iii.

The third prophet of this group is Micah, prophesying shortly before Sennacherib's campaign against Jerusalem in 701 B.C. Wilst referring to Samaria, he is chiefly concerned with Judah. He was a native of the Judean lowlands (i. 1, 14) and from his knowledge of the countryside as well as of the cities he vigorously condemns agrarian injustice and urban evils, showing strong social sympathies. The culminating message of the historical Micah is found in iii. 12 (cf. Jer. xxvi. 18, 19). This original nucleus (i-iii) is followed by a number of exilic or post-exilic promises of consolation of eschatological character, amongst which we note a passage (iv. 1-3) appearing also in Isaiah (ii. 2-4). This section is followed by another (v. 10-vii. 6) which resembles Micah's teaching and may conceivably be by him, though the tone is different. The most impressive and best-known passage is vi. 6-8, the last-named verse giving the best epitome of prophetic religion which the Old Testament contains—namely, to do justice and to love mercy and to walk humbly with God.

The closing portion of the book (vii. 7-20) resembles many Psalms and is clearly post-exilic.

(*b*) *Divine Transcendence.* The first broad conclusion we reach from actually reading the roll of "Isaiah" is that of a distinct break between cc. xxxix and xl. The chapters from xl onwards to lv were written, not in the eighth, but in the sixth century. They are addressed to a people actually in exile under the Babylonians, to people, in fact, in the condition of those carried into captivity in 586 B.C. (2 Kings xxv. 11). They comfort a depressed people with the prospect of speedy deliverance through a great conqueror, who is actually named in xliv. 28, xlv. 1, his victorious career in Asia Minor (about 546) being clearly indicated. We know that this conqueror of the sixth century did overthrow Babylon, fulfilling this prophecy, in 538 B.C. The remaining chapters, lvi-lxvi, detach themselves from this period; they were mostly written in Palestine, and probably during the next century.

We are accordingly left with cc. i-xxxix. Of these, the last four, xxxvi-xxxix, at once detach themselves as a historical appendix, being a transcript of chapters found in our present Second Book of Kings, here quite naturally reproduced because they deal with the work of the prophet Isaiah. This implies that, at one time, the roll of "Isaiah" went no further than xxxv, and so confirms the conclusions we have already reached in regard to xl ff.

When we examine these thirty-five chapters, we find unmistakable signs that they are not a unity, but a collection of collections like the Book of Psalms. The first chapter has a title, "The vision of Isaiah the son of Amoz, which he saw concerning Judah and Jerusalem," etc., which might cover i-xii, but would not cover the foreign prophecies which begin at xiii. Further, we get a second title in ii. 1. This implies that, at some period, ii-iv, with or without v, circulated separately, for at ch. vi, a new beginning is made, in the first person. This autobiographic portion, which extends at least as far as viii. 18, may have been the nucleus of the present first group of twelve chapters, which is rounded off by the post-exilic section, xi. 10–xii. 6. Clearly a passage which speaks of gathering the dispersed of Judah from the four corners of the earth (xi. 12) cannot have been written before the dispersion which it presupposes to have taken place.

The second main section of the Book begins at xiii and extends to xxiii. It is obviously of quite different character, as it relates almost wholly to peoples other than Judah; it is a collection of foreign prophecies, such as we find for example in the Book of Jeremiah (xlvi-li). A peculiar feature of this is that it contains ten pieces (with that in xxx. 6, 7) each bearing the title "Oracle" (R.V. "burden"). Apparently, the collection was originally a "Book of Oracles," and such portions as do not bear this title may have been added subsequently. The first of these foreign prophecies is called "the oracle of Babylon," and to this the words seem to have been added "which Isaiah the son of Amoz saw" (xiii. 1). Such a title would not have been necessary had these otherwise anonymous oracles from the first followed i-xii. (It is like a new title page half-way through a printed volume.) Many of these oracles show by their contents, like the first, that they date from the exile or later, and cannot be by Isaiah; the portions which may reasonably be assigned to him are xiv. 28-32 ("Against the Philistines," which is uniquely dated, "In the year that king Ahaz died was this oracle"), xvii. 1-11 ("The Coming Destruction of Syria and Ephraim"), xvii. 12-14 ("The Uproar of Peoples stilled"), xviii. 1-7 ("The Ethiopian Envoys"), xx ("Egypt and Ethiopia to be captives to Assyria"), xxii. 1-14 ("The Valley of Vision"), xxii. 15-25 ("Shebna and Eliakim")—about one-fifth of the whole, whilst in i-xii not more than one-tenth is clearly *not* by Isaiah. The next section of the present Book (xxiv-xxvii) is without any title; it is an apocalypse, which probably belongs somewhere about 300 B.C., four centuries after the time of Isaiah. With xxviii, though there is again no title, we enter on a new section which extends to xxxiii. Internal evidence shows that these chapters for the most part belong to the time of Sennacherib, and are Isaianic. Cc. xxxiv, xxxv, are post-exilic. So far, then, as the work of the historic Isaiah is concerned, we are confined to the first twelve chapters, together with xxvii-xxxiii, and some smaller part of the "Book of Oracles," the "foreign" prophecies.

Within these parts of the book there are two passages that help us to understand how they came to be written, and throw light on the origin of written, as opposed to oral, prophecy—viz., viii. 16-18, and xxx. 8. The former seems to be the conclusion of the autobiographical record found in vi-viii. 18, and reads: "(I will) tie up the testimony (and) seal the teaching in (?) my disciples. And I will wait for Yahweh who hideth his face from the House of Jacob, and I will look for him. Behold, I and the children whom Yahweh hath given to me are for signs and portents in Israel from Yahweh of Hosts who dwelleth in Mount Sion" (Gray). Isaiah's elder son is symbolically called "Remember shall return," meaning that though Ephraim shall perish, Judah, or a portion of Judah, shall (religiously) return to Yahweh and be saved. The nucleus of this remnant

97

may be seen in Isaiah's own disciples, to whom is committed the written record of these things—i.e., presumably the autobiography of which we have some part surviving in vi-viii. 18. Isaiah's own name means "Yahweh has saved," and he may be referring to that when he speaks of himself as a sign and a portent. The point of interest for us is to see why this record, doubtless the first nucleus of collected Isaianic prophecy, came to be written at all. It was because the spoken testimony was rejected; the writing was a sign and a portent like the other writing of the name of Maher-shalal-hash-baz (viii. 1). The sign given by Yahweh is fulfilled without faith in Him being won—except from the little band of faithful followers. As Buchanan Gray says, there is here "an important epoch in the history of religion—the emergence of a spiritual, as distinct from a national, religious society; Isaiah, unlike Amos and Hosea, is not a voice crying unheeded; his distinction lies less in the doctrine of the remnant than in the practical step of creating the remnant in which he believed." (*I.C. Commentary*, p. 155.)

The other passage, xxx. 8, is of similar meaning, and occupies a similar place. Just as the writing named in viii. 16 gives us the clue to the creation of a nucleus of Isaianic records in the crisis of the Syro-Ephraimitic war, so this gives us a similar nucleus for the crisis at the other end of Isaiah's life—the invasion of Sennacherib. As we have seen, xxviii-xxxi relate to this event, and describe the opposition of Isaiah to reliance upon Egypt against Assyria; since men will not believe that Yahweh's help is sufficient, he is bidden "Now go, write it before them on a tablet, and inscribe it in a book, that it may be for the time to come, for ever and ever."

As truly as did Amos and Hosea, Isaiah holds that morality is essential to true religion, but his characteristic emphasis is on the "holiness" of Yahweh—i.e., His separateness from man (cf. Isa. xxxi. 1-3), the so-called "numinous" element. Thus he makes holiness ethical for the first time, and lifts moral requirements of God into a realm of exalted ideas and sanctions. With this emphasis naturally goes that on "faith," also characteristic of this prophet. For the first time in Israel's religious history, faith in God's sufficiency is made cordial to true religion (cf. vii. 9, xxviii. 16). The ground of this is the divine purpose, which cannot fail. That purpose requires a people—hence the doctrine of the inviolability of Zion, whatever the heathen may threaten. Yahweh is the God of history—that is Israel's confidence; the want of faith in Him is due to spiritual blindness: "Ye looked not unto him that had done this, neither had ye respect unto him that fashioned it long ago" (xxii. 11).

(c) *The Day of the Lord*. Faith in the God of history, as illustrated from Isaiah, already involves expectation of "the Day of Yahweh" (e.g., Isa. ii. 11-21). Originally this denoted the day of battle when "Yahweh of hosts" overthrew the enemies of Israel (cf. Ex. xv. 21 with Ps. xliv. 9). Amos lifted this early idea to a new level when he made it the day of universal and moral judgment (cf. v. 18-20 with cc. i, ii). The idea is illustrated by the "Enthronement of Yahweh" Psalms (see p. 143), and around it gathered many eschatological ideas, often expressed in terms drawn from mythology (see under "Apocalyptic"). The idea is strongly emphasized in the three prophets next to be noticed.

After Isaiah, prophecy is silent during the long reign of Manasseh, which was marked by pagan reaction from Yahwism. Then, in the remaining third of the seventh century, we come to a new and vigorous prophetic movement in which figure Jeremiah and three contemporaries. This movement was a reaction from the paganism, and was elicited by the signs of growing weakness in Assyria, notably the invasion of the Scythians about 630 B.C.

Zephaniah, the first of the three, is in particular the prophet of the Day of the Lord, and his prophecy has inspired the great mediæval Latin hymn "Dies iræ." After a title which dates the book in the time of Josiah (638-608), and possibly makes the prophet the fourth descendant from King Hezekiah, the opening paragraph describes the complete destruction which the Day of Yahweh will bring, and its eradication of the existent idolatry and paganism. Then Yahweh's sacrifice is described, a sacrifice in which the victims are the wicked in Judah, the guests apparently being the Scythians. The classes indicated as about to be punished are three—the court, so servile to foreign fashion in religion, the merchants who care for nothing but the wealth destined to be a spoil to the enemy, and the indifferent who say, "Yahweh will not do good, neither will He do evil." Then, after describing in grim terms the gloom and terror of this coming judgment, the prophet turns in the second chapter to the judgment on the Philistines, though he does not specify any reason nor make his threatenings moral, like Amos. (The reference to Moab and Ammon seems to be an exilic insertion, based on remembrance of the attitude of these peoples when Jerusalem fell in 586.) The judgment then falls on Ethiopia and Assyria, and the overthrow of Nineveh is announced.

The opening verses of the third chapter return to Jerusalem, and denounce her princes, judges, prophets, priests. The rest of the chapter (*vv.* 8-20) is devoted to a quite different aspect of Yahweh's intervention, and may possibly be from a later hand, seeking to relieve the unrelieved gloom of Zephaniah's message, just as did the appendix to Amos. As this portion stands, it describes the kingdom of God—without any "Messianic" Prince—which God will establish on earth for the righteous remnant of Judah, when the wicked have been purged away. The regenerate Israel will then become a centre of attraction for the peoples of the world.

It was probably towards 612, when the Babylonians, Medes, and Scythians were attacking Nineveh, that Nahum prophesied. He saw the beginning of the end, and he saw it accurately. He welcomed it with an almost savage delight as the vengeance of God upon the oppressor of God's people, Israel.

The first chapter of the book of Nahum is a poem in which the acrostic or alphabetic form can be traced at least down to the tenth verse. It is a suitable introduction, for it strikes the note of the avenging God, but the probability is that it does not come from Nahum himself, but has been prefixed at a later date. In the second and third chapters we have a vigorous, and even brilliant description of the assault on Nineveh, and its downfall. We see the approach of the assaulters, and the ironical advice to Nineveh to

guard the ramparts against them. The crimson cloaks
of the soldiers and the glittering steel of armour upon
the chariots arrest the eye: they force their way into
the streets, and go jolting along them; the defenders
stumble in their defence; the covering mantelet is
brought up to the walls; the gates of the city, de-
fended by ramparts and moats, lie open. There is
mourning and wailing from the women, beating on
their breasts; the people flow out of the city as water
overflows from a pool, and there is no stopping the
rout. The wealthy city, stored with the plunder of
generations, is itself open to be plundered, and becomes a city of desolation, a lions' den, from which
the lions have gone. Nineveh is like a harlot punished
for her immorality by exposure and shame. Her
warriors have become women; the frantic labours to
repair the breaches in the wall by making new bricks
is futile; the leaders are scattered. And the passage
closes on the note of pitiless vengeance: "There is no
healing for thy wound; thy hurt is incurable; every
one who hears the report of thee claps his hands."

Nahum, then, is the prophet of vengeance, and
of vengeance against a foreign oppressor. If we contrast the prophecy of Nahum concerned with
vengeance on Nineveh with the human pleading for
Nineveh which characterizes the Book of Jonah, we

gain a striking example of the contrasts that lie, often unregarded, within the covers of our Bible.

Habakkuk is the third of Jeremiah's contemporaries. The first section of his book (to ii. 4) seems to refer to the time when the Babylonians had replaced the Assyrians as overlords of Palestine—i.e., after the battle of Carchemish in 605 B.C. This part is in the form of a dialogue between the prophet and God, though there is perhaps some confusion in the present order, and i. 5-11, referring to the Babylonians, would more naturally follow i. 1-4, 12–ii. 4, which denounces the wickedness of Israel, on whom the "Chaldeans" are commissioned to execute the divine penalty, as the answer to the prophet's appeal in ii. 1. It is likely that this earlier prophecy has been expanded and brought up to date by reference to Greek oppression at a later time (the Hebrew word for "wine" in ii. 5 is almost identical with that for "Greek," and this yields much better sense). The "Woes" which form the second part of the book (ii. 5-20) in any case refer to a later period and point to the decline of Babylonian power before the Persians (c. 540 B.C.). The striking poem which forms the third part is quite distinct from the rest, and its liturgical notes suggest that it has been added from some collection like our Book of Psalms. It rises towards the close to a very lofty level of confidence in God, in spite of all adversity. This links it to some extent with the complaint about the suffering of the innocent (within Israel) in the earlier part of the book.

(*d*) *Corporate Individualism.* Jeremiah is preeminently the prophet of "corporate individualism." This does not mean an individualism in sharp antithesis to the previous "corporate personality," but rather an emphasis on the individual *within* the social group, and an emphasis that springs from the personal fellowship with God which this prophet experienced in so marked a degree. He was, in fact, driven in upon God by the isolation resulting from his unpopularity. He stood alone (except for Baruch) in the latter part of his work, as counselling surrender to Babylon. He did this as a direct result of his faith in Yahweh's purpose, whilst Isaiah's similar confidence in the divine purpose had led him to a directly opposite result—viz., the conviction of the inviolability of Jerusalem.

A review of the contents of Jeremiah shows that the main body of the book, i.e., i-xlv, falls into two distinct parts, the first (i-xxv) chiefly prophetic, and written in the first person, the second (xxvi-xlv) chiefly narrative, and written (about Jeremiah) in the third person. The narrative of xxxvi shows us that through the failure of the oral testimony of Jeremiah, he was led to write down his prophecies of the previous twenty-two years, viz. 626-604, hoping even yet for Judah's repentance. Almost all of the first ten chapters, and some considerable part of the following chapters, may be regarded as forming the contents of the roll of 604/3. The closing portion of the book (xlvi-li) consists of "foreign" prophecies. Did any of these belong to the roll of 604/3? We have grounds for expecting that Jeremiah had something to say to, or about, the surrounding peoples, besides the natural probabilities, and the analogy of other prophets—e.g., Amos and Isaiah. Thus in i. 5 we read, "I have appointed thee a prophet unto the nations," since it was impossible to separate the fate of this little kingdom from the history of its neighbours. Again, in i. 10, Yahweh says to Jeremiah, "I have this day set thee over the nations and over the kingdoms, to pluck up and to break down, and to destroy and to overthrow; to build, and to plant." (The Hebrew verb for "set thee" means "made thee an overseer," such as a prophet with wide horizon would necessarily be.) Still further, we notice in xxv, the chapter in which Jeremiah reviews his ministry in the year of the writing of the first roll, that the advance of the Babylonians is figuratively described as a cup of fury given to the nations to drink (15); "Take the cup of the wine of this fury at my hand, and cause all the nations, to whom I send thee, to drink it." In this chapter a specific list of the nations in view is given (19-26); Egypt, Philistia, Edom, Moab, Ammon, Tyre, Sidon, and Mediterranean (Dedan, Tema, Buz, etc.), Elam (and Media), Babylon (Sheshach). How many of these prophecies, then, could have been included in the roll? For we see from xxxvi. 2, that the roll did include some prophecies "against all the nations." The longest of all—viz., the prophecy against Babylon (l. 1–li. 58) —presupposes the destruction of Jerusalem as a remote event of the past, and its ideas of the place and office of Babylon is quite different from Jeremiah's, though Jeremiah's writings seem to have been freely used by the writer. C. xlviii (Moab) also can hardly be by Jeremiah; it incorporates material found in Isa. xv, xvi, an elegy of the fifth century. Much of what remains may be Jeremianic, and may have stood upon the roll.

So far we have been concerned with the probable contents of the roll of 604/3, which we may regard as the first stage in the compilation of the present Book of Jeremiah. The second is that of additions to this roll, consisting of obviously or probably later prophecies—viz., those that refer to the later years of Jehoiakim (e.g., xxii. 13-19), and the reigns of Jehoiachin (xiii. 18, 19, xxii. 20-30) and Zedekiah (e.g., xxi. 1-10, xxiii. 9-40, xxiv).

We have seen that xxvi-xlv consist mainly of narratives about Jeremiah, some of them with connected prophecies, but forming rather a biography of the prophet than a collection of his utterances, such as we found in the first half. We have seen Baruch in xxxvi acting as the secretary of Jeremiah. He appears also in xxxii. 12-16, in connexion with the purchase of land in Anathoth, and in xliii. 3-6, where he is blamed by the Jews as the evil genius of Jeremiah, inspiring him to his "unpatriotic" attitude. In xlv there is an interesting prophecy devoted to Baruch's personal need. In view of this close connexion and its character, it is reasonable to suppose that the biography was written by Baruch. A connected account does not begin before xxxvii. 12 (Jeremiah arrested when leaving Jerusalem); here the detailed incidents confirm the probability that Baruch was the author (note that Jeremiah's prophecy directed to him is put at the end of the narrative). We cannot think that we have the narrative in the order in which he wrote it. In view of the disregard of chronological sequence, we must suppose that the present book has been compiled with liberal use of the biography, according to connexions of its subject-matter with the prophecies, as seemed most suitable to the editors.

The influence of Jeremiah on the subsequent religion of Israel has been very great, as we may see from the Book of Psalms. The book which bears the prophet's name is very valuable for the light it throws on the internal history of "the decline and fall of Judah" (so matching the contribution of his spiritual kinsman, Hosea, in regard to the northern kingdom). But even more valuable is the contribution to religion which is made by the autobiographical poems scattered through the earlier part of the book, describing his call (i. 4-10), his mission (i. 11-19), his anxious sympathies (iv. 19, viii. 18 ff., xiii. 17, xxiii. 9), his sense of the power of Yahweh (iv. 23-26), his lonely sorrows (xv. 10-21), the divine compulsion which kept him to his task in spite of its difficulty (xx. 7-18). These constitute the most interesting part of the book, and throw much light on the prophetic consciousness at its highest. They also show the realization of that ideal of an inward personal relation to God in which consists the essence of religion, and explain his attitude towards the "externalism" of dependence on the temple and its worship (vii. 4). He anticipated a time when all would share in the privilege of the prophetic consciousness, and this anticipation finds expression in his culminating prophecy of the "New Covenant" (xxxi. 31-34).

(e) *Sacramentalism.* Ezekiel was a priest as well as a prophet and this explains some of the distinctive features of his prophecy. He was deported to Babylon in 597, that is, amongst the first batch of exiles from the southern kingdom. The vision in the first chapter which constituted his call to prophecy is of a remarkable character. It combines the phenomena of a storm with some of those elaborate combinations of creatures which were employed in Mesopotamian sculpture and temple-symbolism. There is much more of the literary quality about this vision than we find in the case of earlier prophets.

One striking feature in this prophet is the evidence of abnormality in his consciousness and behavior. For example, in iii. 25-27 we have what appears to be the description of a cataleptic state. There were periods when Ezekiel was unable to move or to speak. It would be quite natural for one who had become conscious of a prophetic mission to interpret such physiological conditions as constituting a command of Yahweh, just as we know he interpreted his wife's death (xxiv. 15 ff.). We also find that he had trance states (viii. 1 ff.) combined possibly with powers of television in which, whilst remaining in Babylon, he saw what was going on in the temple at Jerusalem in 591. Further, the symbolic acts of this prophet seem to go beyond those generally wrought by other prophets. This emphasis on "enacted symbolism" together with the equally marked emphasis on the ritual of the temple after its contemplated restoration justify us in regarding him as the most "sacramental" of the prophets.

It need hardly be said that abnormalities of consciousness or behaviour should not be regarded as in any way derogatory to the function of Ezekiel as a prophet. They are no more than the abnormalities which have often accompanied genius in other realms —e.g., Blake.

In the study of Ezekiel's prophetic work the most obvious feature is the sharp division which was made by the siege and fall of Jerusalem (587-6). This divides the book as it stands into almost exact halves, since the news of the siege comes to the prophetic consciousness of Ezekiel at the beginning of ch. xxiv. The fall of the city is actually reported in 585 (see ch. xxxiii. 21), and the news terminates the state of dumbness (aphasia) in which the prophet had previously been. The fulfilment of his warnings sets him free for a different kind of work springing from a different attitude. This is expressed by saying that he was a denunciatory prophet till the fall of the city and a consoling pastor, or, to use his own term, "watchman," after that event. This latter mission may be illustrated by his hope of an inward regeneration (xxxvi. 26 ff., "a new heart also will I give you," etc.; cf. xi. 19) and also of a national resurrection, expressed in the vision of the valley of dry bones (xxxvii. 1-14). In this connexion should be noticed his strong and characteristic emphasis on a new individualism (xiv. 1 ff., xviii. 2 ff., xxxiii. 1-20). If to these two roles—namely, that of prophet and pastor—we add that of priest, seen especially in the closing portion of the book (xl-xlviii), we see what apparent contradictions or at least contrasts there were in his personality. Some account of the priestly "legislation" will be found in Ch. VII (p. 183).

One marked feature of the present Book of Ezekiel is its literary character, since it has been either written or arranged on a definite plan with frequent dates. No other prophet is so consecutive in the arrangement of his book, whether this be due to Ezekiel himself or to his editors. The only part in which it is necessary to suppose that there have been considerable alterations or additions is the last nine chapters, which outline the restored Jewish temple and city. They would naturally lend themselves to expansion and adjustment to the actual conditions of a subsequent age, such as are reflected in the Priestly Code. But it is not only in regard to these anticipations that Ezekiel has been called the father of Judaism. His general religious attitude is much nearer that of a later age than that of his companion prophet Deutero-Isaiah. Ezekiel is also the ancestor of the apocalyptic literature (xxxviii, xxxix). The group of foreign prophecies (xxv-xxxii) matches the similar group which we find in Isaiah and Jeremiah. The peculiar features of the book have led some scholars in recent times to doubt the substantial unity which has been accepted in the foregoing account. But none of the divisions as yet suggested, whether based on time (part written before or after the sixth century) or on place (part written in Jerusalem and part in Babylon) has won general assent.

(*f*) *Evangelism*. We saw that Isaiah xl-lv belongs to the period of exile, at the time when the victories of Cyrus (from 546 onwards) must have aroused hopes of the overthrow of Babylon in many Jewish hearts. One of these exiles, whose name has not come down to us, interpreted these victories as the work of Israel's God (Isa. xli. 2-4) and recognized Cyrus as His "anointed" (xlv. 1). Other reasons for detaching these chapters from the earlier part of the "Book of Isaiah" are (1) their presupposition of exilic events and conditions (xlvi. 1, 2, xlviii. 20); (2) their different characteristic ideas, such as the emphasis on Yahweh's creative work (xl. 28); (3) their style and phraseology, especially the more "literary" character, which suggests that they were written from the beginning to be read rather than spoken. The lack of continuity and progressive development in the succession of the prophecies suggests that they consist of a number of separate pieces composed at different times; but that they have been brought together into some sort of unity seems clear when we compare the opening verses, "Comfort ye," etc., with the closing chapter (lv) which returns to the same key. The direct references to Babylon and Cyrus are found only in the first half (xl-xlviii), for which reason (with other differences) xlix-lv are sometimes ascribed to a later period—e.g., after the fall of Babylon in 538—when the hope of return must have become stronger, though as yet there had been no adequate fulfilment of it.

The dominant theme of "Deutero-Isaiah" is the "comfort" of Israel in exile through the promise of speedy deliverance. This is based chiefly on three grounds: (1) the power of Yahweh over nature (xl. 12 ff.) which guarantees His sufficiency as a delivering God; (2) His actual control of history, as seen in the marvellous career of Cyrus (xli. 2 ff.); (3) His knowledge of the future (xli. 21-29), which springs from that controlling purpose, and stands in sharp contrast with the dumbness of the idols of other "Gods" (xliv. 9 ff.). It is in this prophet that the implicit monotheism of the eighth century first becomes explicit (with Deut. vi. 4, cf. *v.* 14).

The most striking feature of these chapters is, however, the new conception of the mission of Israel

as "the Servant of Yahweh" which is found in four
"songs" (xlii. 1-4, xlix. 1-6, l. 4-9, lii. 13–liii. 12)
more or less detached from their present context, in
which they may have been distributed subsequently
to their composition. They present a clearly drawn
and strongly individualized figure, prophetic in function and method, patient and gentle in spirit, conscious of being a weapon in the divine hand, and sustained by companionship with Yahweh. To him is
given the task of bringing the world to Yahweh's feet,
through the Servant's endurance of undeserved suffering, which attains sacrificial and vicarious value.
This interpretation of innocent suffering is the chief
contribution of the Old Testament to the solution of
the greatest problem in Israel's religion. For the
Christian it is the clearest anticipation of Christ and
His Cross (though it is not to be confused with the
quite different figure of the "Messianic" Son of
David).

Whom does this figure represent? Scholars have
given the most varied answers, ranging from individual men, such as Jeremiah, to Israel as a whole,
conceived collectively. In favour of the latter view,
we must remember the vivid and dramatic way in
which Israel is elsewhere described (cf. Ezekiel xvi
and xxiii) and the fact that in other parts of these
chapters Israel is explicitly named as "the Servant"

(xli. 8, cf. Jer. xxx. 10). We can, however, best explain the variety of interpretation amongst scholars by the Hebrew conception of "corporate personality," which here, as in many Psalms, allows rapid transition from the whole group to any single or representative member of it—a way of thinking for which there is no exact modern parallel: Israel *is* meant, but Israel as represented by its men of prophetic spirit, who have learnt to make an offering to God of their own and the nation's sufferings.

(g) *The Decline and Fall of Prophecy.* Deutero-Isaiah was the last of the great prophets; the exile rules a line across the religion of Israel in this, as in so many other respects. There was prophecy in the Persian period, but it is distinctly of a lower order, and in the Greek period prophecy falls into disrepute and disappears.

The building of the second temple was due to the initiative of Haggai (520) and Zechariah (i-viii; 520-518). They stirred up from their lethargy the religious and civil leaders, and the people, whether continuous residents in Judea or newly returned exiles. Haggai argued that the adversities from which the colony was suffering were directly due to neglect to rebuild the temple, and when the initial difficulties of the actual attempt brought despondency, he promised greater glory for the second temple than for the first, through the inflow of wealth from the nations (ii. 6-9). This expectation was bound up with the Messianic hope; Zerubbabel the governor was of the royal house, the grandson of Jeconiah, and could therefore be hailed as the Messianic prince (ii. 23; cf. Jer. xxii. 24). The political basis of this hope was the series of rebellions which threatened to overthrow the Persian Empire, at the time of the accession of Darius.

A couple of months after Haggai had begun to prophesy, Zechariah (i-viii only) called the people to repentance, and shortly afterwards experienced the "night visions" (i. 7–vi. 8) which are characteristic of him. These are, the horsemen reporting that the Messianic crisis still lingers on the way (i. 7-17), the cutting down of the four horns, representing the heathen powers of the world (i. 18-21), the city too large for walls, but divinely protected (ii. 1-13), the acquittal of the high-priest, representing Judah (iii. 1-10), the seven-branched lampstand, representing the watchful eyes of Yahweh, and the two olive trees (Joshua and Zerubbabel; iv. 1-14), the flying roll bringing its "automatic" curse on thieves and false-swearers, which cleanses the land (v. 1-4), the removal of the woman representing the guilt of the land (v. 5-11), and finally the long-awaited mission of the chariots to execute judgment on the heathen (vi.

1-8). The incident of the making of the crowns (vi. 9-15) seems originally to have referred to Zerubbabel alone and the Messianic princedom. Two years after the night visions there is a divine oracle that the fasts which have been kept through the exile shall become festivals, and the happiness of the coming Messianic age is portrayed (vii, viii). It is evident that the directness of the prophetic fellowship with God has now been lost, for there is an interpreting angel for these visions and the initial reference to the former prophets shows that the classic age of prophecy is now past.

The book of Malachi is really anonymous; its name transliterates the Hebrew word for "my messenger" (iii. 1). The main topics of the prophecy are the neglect of the cult, for which the priests are responsible (i. 6-14, ii. 1-9), and the divorce of native wives for the sake of marriage with foreigners (ii. 10-16). Upon the moral indifference and religious unbelief judgment is at hand (ii. 17–iii. 6), when there will be a sharp discrimination between the ungodly and the godly (iii. 13–iv. 3). The passage now found between the last two—viz., iii. 7-12, which declares that the renewal of prosperity will depend on the payment of tithe—may originally have followed i. 1-5, which contrasts some recent disaster on the hated Edom with Yahweh's love for Israel. The most probable date for this prophecy is about the middle of the fifth century, shortly before the work of Nehemiah, whose reforms suggest similar conditions. Obviously the temple has been rebuilt (i. 10, iii. 1, 10), and the reference to the "governor" (i. 8) implies the Persian period. Two notable passages in the book are i. 11, showing an unusually broad recognition of Gentile worship, and iii. 16, which shows the formation of an inner religious group, or "church," distinct from the nation. The concluding reference to Moses and Elijah, which was so influential on later belief and expectation, forms an impressive close to "The Book of the Twelve," and to the Old Testament in the order of the English Bible.

The short prophecy of Obadiah may refer to the same disaster that has befallen Edom and may therefore in *vv*. 1-14 belong to the same period as "Malachi"—i.e., *c*. 450 B.C. But *vv*. 15-21 are of different origin and proclaim the eschatological "Day of Yahweh." It should be noted also that the first five verses of the prophecy reappear in Jeremiah xlix. 14-16, and *v*. 9; cf. also Joel ii. 32 with Obadiah *v*. 17.

The eleven chapters which follow Deutero-Isaiah —viz., Isaiah lvi-lxvi (often called "Trito-Isaiah")— are of different occasions and in all probability by different hands at different times. The unity which characterized Deutero-Isaiah is conspicuously lacking:

(1) lvi. 1-8. Proselytes and eunuchs are welcomed to the community of Israel.

(2) lvi. 9–lvii. 2. The hostile nations are bidden to attack Israel, whose rulers are incompetent; meanwhile good men die.

(3) lvii. 3-13. A community, apparently living in Palestine (5-7; note the topography), is bitterly attacked for its heathenism, which is futile (this may refer to the "Samaritans," or their Jewish supporters).

(4) lvii. 14-21. Yahweh promises his presence with the devout, and peace to those near and to those far—i.e., to dwellers in Jerusalem and to exiles in other lands.

(5) lviii. A prophetic demand for spiritual rather than ritual fasting, for the practical righteousness of loosing captives, feeding the hungry, recognizing the claims of social brotherhood. This will secure a response from Yahweh, and the waste places shall be built. (Two quite different verses at the end add a demand for the keeping of the Sabbath.)

(6) lix. Further denunciation of the people's sins, which are the real cause of Yahweh's standing aloof. This the people themselves confess (9 ff.), whereupon Yahweh manifests himself in a theophany as an armed warrior (15*b*-end).

(7) lx-lxii.   A glowing description of the restoration and future glory of Zion (which comes nearest to Deutero-Isaiah and is ascribed by some to him). Ch. lxi begins with a passage apparently modelled on the Servant of Yahweh Songs ("The Spirit of Yahweh is upon me").

(8) lxiii. 1-6.   A dramatic picture of Yahweh as a blood-stained warrior, coming back from executing vengeance on Edom.   (This suggests a date near Malachi i. 2-5 and Obadiah—i.e., *c*. 450, unless it is eschatological, with Edom as the typical enemy.)

(9) lxiii. 7–lxiv.   A liturgy of thanksgiving for Yahweh's providence in the past (7-14); a prayer for His present intervention, and a confession of unworthiness.   [This seems to imply (lxiv. 10, 11) that the temple is still unbuilt after its destruction—i.e., this passage must be dated before 516, though after 586.]

(10) lxv, lxvi.   Vengeance on those who practise idolatrous and heathenish rites; promises of mercy and help for the true servants of Yahweh.   The happy time of restoration for Yahweh's people is pictured. Scorn is expressed for the building of a temple to the God of heaven (lxvi. 1 f.; was this a rival temple projected by the Samaritans?).   The new nation will be miraculously born (7), the servants of Yahweh will be blessed, and all the nations will bring their

offerings to Jerusalem. The book ends with a picture of the fate of evil-doers, made a spectacle to the righteous.

It will be seen how impossible it is to sum up these miscellaneous contents, which seem to range from the time of Exile down to that of Ezra and Nehemiah at least. The historical, social, and geographical background, where there is any evidence at all, seems to be Palestine (lvii. 5-7 for the land; lvi. 9 ff. for native rulers). The emphasis on the Sabbath (lvi. 6, lviii. 13, 14) suggests a post-exilic date, and the time of Nehemiah. The Temple (for the most part) seems to be standing, though the walls of the city do not seem to be built (lx. 7 and 10). Language and style mostly confirm the difference of authorship suggested by the range of ideas. We seem to see a community in the position of Jerusalem before the work of Ezra and Nehemiah, with the two factions of the pro-heathen or "Samaritan," trying to combine various religious rites with the worship of Yahweh, and a Puritan party, which goes back to the influence of Ezekiel. The broad and generous outlook towards the nations seen in Deutero-Isaiah is mostly wanting here.

"Joel" begins with the description of a contemporary calamity, consisting of an unprecedented plague of locusts, which has destroyed vegetation so completely that even the meal-offerings and the

drink-offerings for the daily sacrifices fail (i. 9, 13).
The prophet interprets this calamity as the advance-
guard of the forces of the Day of Yahweh (i. 15),
and urges the people to keep a fast, and make petition
to Yahweh; the locusts are accompanied by a drought
(i. 19, 20), unless the writer means to describe the
effects of the plague of locusts by this figure. In the
second chapter, he continues the same theme, describing the locusts as an invading army, and developing
the accompanying signs of the Day of Yahweh, in a
fashion that makes it difficult to decide where the real
and the ideal meet. In the second half of the prophecy (ii. 18 ff.), comes the reply of Yahweh, who
promises to renew fertility and expel the invading
locusts (19, 20). Let the land and its occupants re-
joice in the rain which comes as the prelude to this
fertility (21-24). The years which the locust has
eaten shall be restored. But the restoration opens up
into a manifestation of Yahweh's grace beyond experience (28 ff.). He promises to pour out His spirit
on the whole people of Judah, so that they shall share
in the prophetic consciousness of God (28, 29).
Supernatural signs will usher in the Day of Yahweh,
when Yahweh-worshippers will be saved—i.e., true
Israelities; whilst the nations of the earth are to be
judged (iii. 1 ff.), more particularly those neighbouring peoples who have showed such unneighbourly

conduct—viz., Phœnicians and Philistines (iii. 4 f.), though Egypt and Edom also are subsequently named (19, 20). The charge brought against the Phœnicians and Philistines is that they have robbed Israel of gold and silver, and have sold Israelites as slaves to the Greeks, in return for which they shall themselves be sold to the Sabeans (8). The heathen nations may gather to the fray as they will, but Yahweh sits as judge in the valley of decision, where their noisy multitudes are assembled (14). Yahweh shall roar from Zion, heaven and earth quake, His people be rescued, and the stranger will no longer pass through Jerusalem. Jerusalem's future prosperity is assured forever, and the innocent blood shed in the past will be avenged.

The date of Joel's prophecy, in the light of internal evidence, may be about 400 or possibly later. There is silence as to the powers which were on the horizon of the pre-exilic prophets—viz., the Syrians, the Assyrians, the Babylonians. Judah and Jerusalem alone are in his thought; Israel no longer exists for him; Judah has been scattered and its sons killed or enslaved; the temple treasures have been plundered by surrounding peoples. On the other hand, the temple has been rebuilt and its services have been resumed, though there is no king. There are many literary parallels with earlier prophets, parallels which show that Joel is the probable borrower. There can be no doubt therefore that the prophecy belongs to the time after Haggai and Zechariah, and there seems much probability that it falls after Malachi, whose reference to "the great and terrible day of Yahweh" (iv. 5) seems to be quoted in Joel ii. 31. Besides this, the apocalyptic outlook seen in the working up of the detail of the Day of Yahweh, so fully pictured here, seems to imply a relatively late date. On the other hand, iv. 4 ff. (E.T. iii. 4 f.) and iv. 19 (E.T. iii. 19) show that the enemy are not yet the Greek powers (Seleucids and Ptolemies), so that we must put the book before the time of Alexander. (The reference to the Greeks in iii. 6 (E.T.) does *not* imply a date after Alexander.) Altogether, we get in Joel an interesting glimpse of the development of religion and social life in the later Persian period, of which we know so little from outside sources. The Book of Joel marks the transition from prophecy to apocalyptic. (For an analysis of the obscure and partly apocalyptic Zech. ix–xiv, see the Appendix.)

Though there are great passages in the prophecies we have just been reviewing, expressing permanent truth in memorable form, we cannot but feel that post-exilic prophecy moves from the very beginning on a lower level than that of its predecessors. These later prophets are themselves nearer to the level of those they address, and often seem rather to express the thoughts of the people themselves. The power is passing from the prophet to the priest, even though priests are rebuked by some of these prophets. It is rather striking that the last public appearance of prophecy in narrative should be in the persons of the prophets of whose machinations Nehemiah complains (vi. 10-14). But the last actual mention of prophecy is found in the latter part of Zechariah, belonging to the Greek period. God, it is said, will cleanse the land from *the prophets and the unclean spirit* (Zech. xiii. 2). The contemporary prophet is disowned even by his parents, and made ashamed of his vision and of his garb of deceit, forced to save himself from popular indignation by saying that he is not a prophet, and bearing wounds which he has received in the house of his friends. Truly a strange ending of the movement which was Israel's greatest glory; *corruptio optimi pessima.*

(*h*) *The Contribution of Prophecy to the Religion of Israel.* The main principles of the prophetic teaching can be gathered under four heads—viz., the ideas of God, of sin and judgment, of grace and salvation, and of the interpretation of history.

The prophetic idea of God is known as "ethical monotheism," by which is meant that the emphasis on the moral nature of Yahweh universalized Him be-

yond all nationalistic limits: "the prophets unhesitat-
ingly placed righteousness and not race as the first
ground of Yahweh's action" (Buchanan Gray).
They fully retained His personality, and their idea
was very different from the monotheistic speculations
of Babylonia or Egypt. The earlier conceptions of the
God of Sinai, of the ark in the camp, of the sanctuaries of Canaan, of the starry hosts, of Urim and
Thummim, all contributed to the ultimate majesty of
the one God of all the earth whose "holiness" had become His moral quality.

The sins they condemned in His name are partly
breaches of the corporate personality of Israel, the
violence, falsehood, and sensuality of common life,
the social injustice springing from greed for possessions, the professional selfishness and insincerity that
degraded prophecy and the priesthood, the luxury that
enervated manhood and womanhood; partly they are
direct disloyalties to Yahweh—viz., the political al-
liances with Assyria or Egypt that showed distrust of
Yahweh, the assiduous ritual of His worship that had
no care for His moral requirements, the resort to
idolatry that was comparable with a breach of the
marriage bond and materialized the very idea of God.
These rampant sins will be punished as they deserve in
that always imminent judgment which is called "The
Day of Yahweh," a judgment to be wrought partly

by human agents and partly by the more direct action of Yahweh.

The emphasis of the pre-exilic prophets falls on sin and judgment, but the ideas of grace and salvation are almost always present, even where we have fully allowed for later additions under this head. The very threat of punishment is implicitly a call for repentance and an opportunity for it. There is to be a happy future for the righteous, because penitent and sifted, remnant. The great saving acts of God in the past will be renewed in the future, and the "Messianic" hope represented in some of the books, whatever its date of emergence, means the establishment of a divine kingdom upon the earth, often under a prince of divinely given equipment.

Finally, they were the first to conceive human history as a unity controlled by a divine purpose. History is the story of God's dealings with men, and the principle of its unity is seen in the covenant made at Sinai, by which Israel is elect amongst the nations to fulfil the purpose of Yahweh. But divine control did not lessen the moral responsibility of men. All Hebrews were realists; they lived intensely and believed that God as well as man was known by His acts. The prophets gave to the reality of human life not an eternal significance—for "eternity" was not amongst their ideas—but a moral and religious significance that

has no parallel outside the spiritual heirs to prophetic
teaching—viz., Jesus and His disciples.

4. *Apocalyptic.* The most direct descendant of
prophecy was apocalyptic, not only because the presupposition of both is the same—viz., the imminence
of judgment, but also because apocalyptic may be said
to have had its beginning in unfulfilled prophecy (so
Charles, *Eschatology*, p. 106; cf. Ezek. xxxviii. 14-
17). The Book of Joel describes the "Day of Yahweh" in thoroughly apocalyptic terms (ii. 28 ff.).
The last three chapters of the Book of Zechariah (belonging, like cc. ix-xi, to the Greek period) are also
apocalyptic. There is an apocalypse contained in the
present Book of Isaiah—viz., xxiv-xxvii (*c.* 300 B.C.).
The most important Old Testament example of this
genre is, however, the second part (cc. vii ff.) of the
Book of Daniel. A large number of apocalyptic
books help to bridge the apparent but not real gulf
between the Old and New Testaments, from Enoch to
4 Ezra.

Apocalyptic differs from prophecy, however,
both in content and in form. In apocalyptic, the
prophetic interpretation of contemporary history is
extended to embrace all the generations according to
some fixed scheme which is supposed to be revealed in
advance to an elect man. This is usually some great
figure of the past—Adam, Enoch, Abraham, Moses,

etc.—who is permitted to see all future history un-rolled before his eyes, in a vast panorama (cf. the similar vision in Israel's history given to Moses on Pisgah, according to Jewish commentators). This vision extends, however, beyond the earth to heaven and hell, and the emphasis falls indeed on resurrection and the blessed life after death.

The chief difference of form between prophecy and apocalyptic is the excessive use of conventional-ized symbolism and traditional phraseology which the apocalyptic employs. The symbolic acts of the prophets are replaced by elaborate zoological and mythological figures; the sense of direct personal con-tact with God and of divine guidance has been lost, though there is doubtless a psychology of apocalyptic inspiration, as well as of prophetic; the apocalyptist may have felt himself actually identified with the great man whose name he employed, just as Elisha asked that an eldest son's portion of Elijah's spirit might inspire him (2 Kings ii. 9).

A good impression of the standard features of apocalyptic may be gained from reading Isaiah xxiv-xxvii. Here there is a description of the universal judgment which is close at hand (xxiv. 1-20), the punishment of heavenly and earthly rulers (xxiv. 21, 22), the visible glory of Yahweh established in Zion (xxiv. 23), and His coronation festival (xxv. 6-8).

During the time of wrath His people withdraw into safety (xxvi. 20–xxvii. 1), and finally the Jews of the Dispersion are recalled to Jerusalem (xxvii. 12-13). It should be noted that the doctrine of resurrection (of the good only) here appears for the first time (xxvi. 19). The catholicity of spirit in xxv. 6-8 is also noteworthy.

The Book of Daniel consists of a narrative part (i-vi) and an apocalyptic (vii-xii). The former may have been a third-century compilation of stories of heroism under persecution, which were incorporated by the author of the apocalypse, itself certainly written at the beginning of the Maccabean revolt (*c.* 165 B.C.). The evidence for this is overwhelming: (1) the book is included amongst the Hagiographa, the third and latest part of the Canon, and ben Sirach, writing *c.* 180, does not know of its existence; (2) there are fifteen Persian and three Greek words; the Aramaic in which ii. 4–vii. 28 is written is later than that of the sixth century and appears to be of second-century type, and the Hebrew is of an age subsequent to Nehemiah: (3) there are historical inaccuracies such as the statement that Belshazzar was the son of Nebuchadrezzar, whilst "Darius the Mede" is unknown to history; (4) the point at which the vision, from being veiled but gen-

erally accurate history, passes into vague prediction
(end of xi) is precisely that of the Maccabean revolt.

The central thought of the apocalyptic portion
(to which the dream in ch. ii properly belongs) is the
establishment of the kingly rule of God over all its
enemies, the final victory of the divine purpose. The
human form ("son of man" = a man) in ch. vii
represents the holy people of God; the animal forms
stand for the four other kingdoms known to the
writer. The doctrine of resurrection, both for good
and evil men, is taught in xii. 2; it is, however, as yet
an abnormal expedient, introduced to deal with outstanding good or evil men whose earlier death had
removed them from the possibility of their due reward or punishment in the present life. The book
shows a remarkable development of angelology, which
is probably due to Persian influences. But its real and
very important significance is that it gathers up the
unique contribution of Israel to the interpretation of
history, and for the first time presents history in its
full extent, as the working out of the purpose of God.
Prophecy and history have here met together, the
eternal righteousness of God and the final peace of
His people have here greeted each other.

CHAPTER V

THE PSALMS

1. The Book of Psalms is one of the most important and at the same time one of the most difficult books of the Old Testament. It is one of the most important because it is an unconscious epitome of the religion of Judaism stated in terms of experience and, therefore, in living utterance. Consequently it has claimed a place in the public worship of the Church and of the Synagogue and in the private devotion of Christians and Jews out of all comparison with any other book. It mirrors post-exilic Judaism, reflecting the results of many lines of development. It is the most varied of the books of the Old Testament, and we may see in it, side by side, four great and perennial antitheses, namely: (1) the sacrificial system and ritual of the Temple and the prophetic protests against the popular reliance on it; (2) faith in the exact retributive justice of God within the limits of earthly life and the perplexities of those who could not be blind to the sufferings of the innocent and the prosperity of the wicked; (3) the nationalistic demand for supremacy or even for vengeance and the universalistic sense of Israel's missionary stewardship for all the world;

(4) recoil from the shadow of death unilluminated by any light of real life beyond the grave, and the dawning conviction of a fellowship with God that virtually displaces death.

The Psalms, however, form a very difficult book, partly because of this great variety. Every psalm has to be considered by itself, and in the great majority of cases it is impossible to find an exact historical background from which to interpret it. Goethe reminded us that no poetry can be written without a definite occasion and a sufficient motive. Exact exegesis requires precise knowledge of author, time, and occasion, and knowledge of these in regard to the individual psalms is usually wanting. This is partly due to the fact that the Book of Psalms has been gathered from collections of sacred poetry employed in public worship through successive generations and freely adapted for this purpose. The result is that the more individual traits have often been eliminated in the shaping of a lyric of individual experience to the needs of a worshipping community. Thus, though the study of the prophets seems at first sight more difficult than that of the Psalms, owing to frequently obscure references to contemporary events, the serious student finds the opposite to be true, since it is usually easier to date prophecies than psalms just because of the historical references.

Since the Psalms in their present form are obviously intended for use in temple worship with musical accompaniment, as the headings frequently indicate, some reference must be made to the music of the Hebrews. This was of a very primitive kind, melodic and not harmonic. Such references as there are to the music of earlier times (2 Sam. vi. 5; Amos v. 23; Isa. xxx. 29), show that music did take a prominent place in religious ceremony, the instruments being those of percussion, such as timbrels, cymbals, and sistra, stringed instruments such as the lyre and harp, and wind instruments such as the trumpet, the horn, and the flute. After the exile the musical part of the temple-service attained great importance and the professional players gained a permanent place in it (1 Chron. xxv). Three guilds are named, those of Asaph, Heman, and Jeduthun. We are not to think of congregational singing in the modern sense (cf. 2 Chron. xxix, 27, 28, "The congregation worshipped, the singers sang, and the trumpeters sounded"). The part taken by the people is represented in such a verse as 1 Chronicles xvi. 36, where all the people say "Amen," and "Hallelujah." They may also have joined in such a refrain as that of Psalm cxxxvi. The chief use of the music would be to mark the rhythm, which, along with parallelism, characterizes Hebrew poetry. The closing psalm of the Psalter implies the participation of priests, levites, and laymen, and mentions six distinct musical instruments.

There has been considerable difference of view amongst scholars as to the precise relation of the Psalms to the cult. Thus Mowinckel barely admits the existence of any psalms not related to the cult in origin. He traces their origin to the temple singers existing from early days. Gunkel, however, recognizes most of the Psalms as being of private and occasional origin, though subsequently gathered and included in the cult. This view seems more probable in view of the great variety of the Psalms.

Another very vexed question closely related to this variety of origin is that of the general date of the Psalms. There has been an increasing tendency in recent years to recognize a larger pre-exilic element in the Psalter. This recognition is based on such evidence as the early existence of analogous compositions among the Babylonians and Egyptians, and the presence of admittedly early religious poetry in other books of the Old Testament and of primitive features in certain psalms, to say nothing of the tradition which assigns so many of the psalms to David. It may freely be admitted that we might expect earlier religious poetry to be found in the Psalms, just as we have earlier laws in the later priestly collections ascribed to Moses and earlier wisdom sayings in the

later collections or discussions ascribed to Solomon.
Thus in Psalm xxiv. 7-10, "Lift up your heads, O ye
gates," etc., may well be a very early processional
song, as xix. 1-6 may be an early nature poem and
Psalms xx and xxi by their references to a king imply
dates under the monarchy. But when we have admitted this, it still remains true that the Psalms now
lie before us as a post-exilic collection adapted for
post-exilic use and that the theology of the book as
a whole is that of the prophetic religion worked out
in the terms of praise and prayer. Now it is impossible to think of the prophets as anything but pioneers,
yet they would not have been pioneers if any considerable body of the Psalms, as we now have them, had
already existed in their times. It would seem, then,
that all we can do is to abandon any attempt to date
individual psalms, while recognizing with Gunkel and
others that certain types of psalm such as the hymns
of praise and the national laments are likely to be
earlier than the individual laments. It still remains
necessary to start with the post-exilic date of the
Psalter as a whole and to assign psalms or parts of
psalms to the pre-exilic period only when internal
evidence may strongly suggest this. In other words,
the Psalter can be safely used as a source book for our
study of post-exilic religion, but not for the pre-exilic.

  2. In its present form the Psalter consists of five

books. The first four are each closed by a doxology. In Book I (i-xli) virtually all the psalms are ascribed to David. In Book II (xlii-lxxii) there is more variety (xlii-xlix Korah, 1 Asaph, li-lxv David, lxvi, lxvii the chief musician, lxviii-lxx David, lxxi anonymous, lxxii Solomon). At the end of this book there is an editorial note, "Finished are the prayers of David the son of Jesse," showing that there was once a collection of Davidic psalms and that some re-arrangement has taken place since. In Book III (lxxiii-lxxxix) there is an Asaph collection (lxxiii-lxxxiii), followed by other psalms ascribed to Korah, David, Heman, and Ethan. Books IV-V are divided by the doxology of cvi. 48 (cf. 1 Chron. xvi. 35, 36). This division, however, does not seem as natural or early as that between the other books and has probably been made to get five books of psalms in correspondence with the five books of the Torah. Within Books IV and V there is a group of "Pilgrim" Psalms, perhaps used by those who went up from the "Dispersion" to worship at Jerusalem on the great feasts, and a now scattered group of Hallelujah Psalms (civ-cvi, cxi-cxiii, cxv-cxvii, cxxxv, cxlvi-cl), chiefly of liturgical character. In Books II and III we have psalms assigned to guilds of temple singers, and these two books also show the remarkable feature that the personal name Yahweh has been largely altered to that of

Elohim. This may be seen by comparing Psalm xiv with the identical Psalm liii, and Psalm xl. 13-17 with the identical Psalm lxx. (The change may have been made by an editor desiring to minimize the use of the sacred personal name in accordance with the general tendency of the later Judaism.) The occurrence of this editorial work in Psalms xlii-lxxxiii, together with other evidence, shows us that the Book of Psalms is a collection of collections, built up, that is to say, from smaller psalters. As for the ascription of psalms to David, it is made in a still larger degree in the Greek version. There does not seem to be sufficient evidence that David wrote religious poetry at all, and if he did, it could hardly have been of that post-prophetic character which we find in our present Book of Psalms. The ascription to him of Psalm xviii in the appendix to 2 Samuel (xxi-xxiv) is not early evidence. The genuinely early evidence of 2 Samuel i. 17 and iii. 33 presents him as a secular rather than as a religious poet (cf. Amos vi. 5).

3. (*a*) The general meaning of the Psalms is best grasped by starting with their fundamental conception—viz., the idea of God, who is characterized by the great attributes of loving-kindness, righteousness, and holiness. Each of these three attributes needs explanation. The word which is usually rendered loving-kindness (*chesed*) really denotes something

like the New Testament conception of "love" (*agape*). It is not so much a sentiment as a principle involving moral obligation. It is the kernel to which the covenant (*berith*) is the shell. Just as *chesed* is the right relation to man within a human social fellowship, so in the relation of God to man, it is the moral bond which unites Him with His people. The second attribute is righteousness, by which is meant conformity to a standard. It is predominantly a forensic term, denoting the status of the man who is pronounced innocent before a tribunal, and it has a wide application to related ideas such as the deliverance or the act which delivers, so that we can speak of the righteousnesses of God, meaning by this His saving acts. The righteousness of God thus means that He will be and do all that conforms to the standard of Israel's God, including the deliverance or salvation of His faithful people. The third attribute is that of holiness, by no means to be confused with moral righteousness. The term "holy," originally meaning perhaps "separate," seems to go back to primitive ideas of taboo and was first used to denote the mystery and terror belonging to the supernatural which set it apart from man. When the great prophets of the eighth century ethicized the conception of God, they did not lose the conception of His mystery and majesty—i.e., the quality which Otto has made familiar to us as the "numinous." So in Isaiah, the "Holy God" means the God of majesty and mystery, and such a thought underlies, eg., Psalm xc. These three are the chief attributes constituting the ethical image-less monotheism of the Psalter, and all the other religious conceptions we have to notice are subordinate to these.

We can best think of these subordinate conceptions as a series of concentric circles beginning with the largest, that of nature, passing to the smaller one of human and especially Israelite history, then that of contemporary society, next, to the temple, which was the centre of post-exilic Judaism; and finally to the personal religion manifested in the temple, but capable of expanding to a national and sometimes even to a universal consciousness. This expansiveness is very important in the study of the Psalms. It is bound up with the idea of corporate personality and possesses a fluidity of reference for which there is no precise modern parallel. In this way we can best explain the perplexing problem of the speaker in many of the Psalms. He may seem to us to be neither an individual nor the representative of a group nor the whole nation, but all three at once, a voice which expands or contracts the scope of its reference from verse to verse.

(*b*) When we study the nature Psalms (viii, xix.

1-6, xxix, lxv, civ, cxlviii), we must picture a very primitive cosmology, a flat earth supported on mounted pillars in the heart of the seas with a solid firmament arching above and supporting the palace of Yahweh, whilst the caverns of Sheol inhabited by the shades are in the depths of the earth. The making of this primitive world is ascribed to Yahweh (cf. Ps. civ and Gen. i), but the terms are often those of primitive mythology, which may be traced back to Babylonian patterns (civ. 7, lxxiv. 12 ff., lxxxix. 10 ff.). There are no "laws of nature" in our modern sense, and God is conceived as ruling the world order much more directly and with the minimum of secondary causes.

(c) The sense of history runs all through the Psalter, but notable examples of its more explicit expression may be found in lxxviii, cv, cvi, cxiv, and cxxxvi. The comparison of cv and cvi will show the difference between simple confidence in the God of ancient history and the further penetration into the moral and retributive side of the historical record. With this constant historical reference on which the faith in a redemptive God is so largely based, we may couple that prospective view which we call eschatology. The future will be accomplished according to the divine purpose, which is the full establishment of the kingly rule of God. A notable group of Psalms describes His enthronement and the universal recognition of His kingship (xlvii, xciii, vcv-c). It has been suggested that this forward look was specially linked to a "New Year's festival" corresponding with that held in Babylon, which kept alive both the mythology of the past and the eschatology of the future. To this circle of ideas belong the so-called Messianic Psalms—e.g., ii, which describe Israel's Davidic king in more or less idealized terms.

(*d*) When we turn to the contemporary social relations of the Psalms, we are impressed by the frequent denunciations of the ungodly and the many "enemies" of the psalmists (cxxxvii, lxxxiii, lix, lviii, lxix, cix). It is clear that they conceive themselves as belonging to an inner community of the pious which feels itself set apart from and superior to its contemporaries. The most natural solution of this feature along the lines of that corporate personality which has just been mentioned is to regard the group thus speaking through its representative as continuing that of Isaiah's disciples (viii. 16; cf. the "Church," as we may call it, of Malachi, iii. 13 ff.). But we have also to remember that the smaller Jewish community settled in and around Jerusalem was constantly exposed to political and social danger in a physical and not simply in a spiritual sense. This doubtless gave the more intensity to the denunciation of national enemies forming the actual environment of the Jewish community. The chief problem which concerned the community of the pious, indeed the chief problem of Israel's religion, was that of the prosperity of the wicked and the adversity of the good (cf. the Book of Job).

(*e*) Passionate devotion to the Temple as the centre of post-exilic Judaism is expressed in many psalms, but reaches its high-water mark in Psalms xlii and xliii, lxxxiv and lxxxvii. It is difficult for us to imagine the noise and colour of the temple worship and the fascination of its now elaborate ritual. But this ritual was the material bond uniting the devout worshipper to God, which gave him a name (*chasid*, the kindly or pious man) cognate with the term (*chesed*) expressing the loving-kindness of God. To this centre came the pilgrims, of whom we get some glimpses in the pilgrimage psalms (cxx. ff., "The Songs of Ascent"). One of the great conceptions of worship is that which makes the worshipper the protected guest of Yahweh (xv and xxiv). It is not until the Maccabean times that we can note the transference of emphasis from the temple ritual to the written law. But this development is reflected in a few law psalms (i, xix. 7-14, cxix).

(*f*) Finally, we may note some qualities of the personal religion which expanded through these concentric circles or contracted to the individuality of the worshipper, who might see in the temple such a vision of God as was granted to Isaiah. The notes of this personal religion were a triumphant trust in Yahweh's help, a deep and penitent humility before Him (Psalm xxxii, li, cxxx; vi, xxxviii, cii, cxliii) combined with a consciousness of "righteousness" in comparison with the heathen peoples round about. Perhaps it was because the outlook was confined to this earth and because no confidence in life beyond death is expressed by the Psalms that the religion was so intense and realistic. It is doubtful whether the Psalms give us any prospect of a real life beyond death other than the mere existence of the shades "who praise not Yahweh." The only probable exception is in the words which have been described as the high-water mark of Old Testament religion—viz., those towards the end of Psalm lxxiii; even here the logic of the faith expressed is not worked out explicitly.

4. *The Book of Lamentations* may be regarded as a special collection of psalms. It consists of five poems, the first four of which have the peculiar rhythm of the longer line followed by a shorter known as the "Kinah" or dirge, whilst they are also written in acrostic form, each verse beginning with a successive letter of the Hebrew alphabet (in iii each verse-line). The fifth poem is of a different kind,

and is really a psalm-like prayer, which may have been written amongst the survivors remaining in Jerusalem, after the fall of the city in 586. It is this event which forms the subject of the first four poems also. Of these ii and iv seem to be by an eye-witness, and are of superior poetical quality to the others; ii dwells on the events of the siege and capture of the city by the Babylonians, with the pathetic picture of little children dying of hunger at their mothers' breasts (11, 12), whilst the fourth strikes a stronger note of indignation [17-20, e.g., "the breath of our nostrils, the anointed of Yahweh (i.e., Zedekiah) was taken in their pits"]. The first and third are more general in character, being without the vivid touches of the second and the fourth, and are probably later in composition. The third has for its notable feature a strongly marked "personification," "I am the man that hath seen affliction by the rod of his wrath" (iii. 1). This "individual lament" is, however, based on the conception of corporate personality, which enables the poet to pass from his own personal sorrows to those of his particular group or of the whole nation; he feels himself the representative and summary of all in their sorrows.

We know nothing of the authorship of these poems. They were ascribed to Jeremiah in the Greek Version (LXX), which has a superscription to that effect, and the same ascription is found in the Targum. But the general attitude of the poems is quite different from that of the prophet; Jeremiah could not have written "her prophets find no vision from Yahweh" (ii. 9), or have spoken of himself as expecting help from Egypt (iv. 17).

CHAPTER VI

THE WISDOM LITERATURE

1. The early idea of "wisdom" was of practical ability or sagacity, as is illustrated by Joseph's character and fitness for the governorship of Egypt—"a man discreet and wise"—and by the sagacity of Solomon in distinguishing between the true and false mother of the child (1 Kings iii. 16-28). As early as the seventh century, there was a more or less distinct class of men in Israel, known as the "wise," who are ranked with priests and prophets. Thus in Jeremiah xviii. 18, we read that national self-confidence expressed itself in the words "the law shall not perish from the priest, nor counsel from the wise, nor the word from the prophet." Another passage from the same prophet suggests that these wise men were more or less identical with the "writers" or scribes: "How do ye say, 'We are wise, and the Torah of Yahweh is with us?' But, behold, the false pen of the writers has wrought falsely" (Jer. viii. 8). This learned class give "counsel," practical advice, just as the prophet delivers an authoritative "word" of Yahweh, and the priest a "law" or traditional rule. Apparently it was from

this class of learned men that the subsequent "Wisdom" writers developed.

The Wisdom literature of the Old Testament consists of three books—viz., Proverbs, Job, and Ecclesiastes. In addition to these three, however, there are two extra-canonical books of this class—viz., Ecclesiasticus (The Wisdom of ben Sirach) and "The Wisdom of Solomon"—of which some notice must be taken to make this chapter complete. Our first concern is with:

2. *The Book of Proverbs*. The word "proverb" amongst ourselves denotes "a short pithy saying in general use," such as "cast ne'er a clout till May be out," which is a sumptuary law for many people. But the Hebrew word translated "proverb"—viz., *Mashal*—is of much wider scope. It denotes a "likeness" or comparison, or symbolic saying, such as the popular remark in the times of Jeremiah (xxxi. 29) and Ezekiel (xviii. 2), "the fathers have eaten sour grapes and the children's teeth are set on edge." But it can be applied to any short popular saying, such as "Is Saul also among the prophets?" (1 Sam. x. 12, xix. 24), or to a longer utterance, such as Ezekiel's allegory of the eagle carrying off the top of a cedar tree to plant it elsewhere, which represents the capture of Jehoiachin by Nebuchadrezzar (Ezek. xvii. 2 ff.).

The Book of Proverbs is *prima facie* a collection

of collections, like the Book of Psalms. This is shown both by the sub-titles, and by the differences of content of the sections thus indicated. If we confine ourselves to the titles, we get seven main divisions, though this must not exclude the possibility that some of these are themselves composite. The *first* is headed:

THE PROVERBS OF SOLOMON THE SON OF DAVID, KING OF ISRAEL

This title covers the first nine chapters, which are evidently a unity, and illustrate the longer type of discussion of moral and religious truth as applied to life. We have here a series of loosely linked discourses on "Wisdom" and its excellence as a guide to conduct.

The *second* section of the book begins with ch. x and extends to xxii. 16. It is headed:

THE PROVERBS OF SOLOMON

These twelve and a half chapters form the central part of the book. They consist of individual proverbs in a brief couplet form, generally based on a contrast, e.g., xvi. 1:

> *To man the plans of the heart,*
> *From Yahweh the answer of the tongue,*

corresponding to our own "man proposes, God disposes." There is no classification by subject, though occasionally some of the same type seem to have strayed together. In this disunity of theme, the second section is quite unlike the first. There are both secular and religious proverbs, and the principle of retribution is strongly emphasized.

The *third* section is brief and has a still briefer appendix. In xxii. 17 we find: "Incline thine ear, and hear the words of the wise." The Greek shows that this was originally headed:

THE WORDS OF THE WISE

Then in xxiv. 23 we find again a title:

THESE ALSO ARE OF THE WISE

which extends to the end of ch. xxiv. This section (with its appendix) is much more of a unity, and more in the manner of the first section. It gives practical advice and warning, as from father to son— e.g., against gluttony and drunkenness and idleness (e.g., the field of the sluggard, xxiv. 30 f.). The first part of this collection (xxii. 17–xxiv. 22) is of special interest in view of the recent discovery of a book of Egyptian Wisdom, known as *The Teaching of Amenophis*, which is probably to be dated about 600

B.C. Between this book and Proverbs xxii. 17–xxiv. 22, there are close likenesses, which indicate common origin—e.g., xxii. 24.

> *Do not associate to thyself a man given to anger,*
> *Nor go in company with a wrathful man,*

for which Amenophis has

> *Do not associate to thyself the passionate man*
> *Nor approach him for conversation.*

One of the most convincing proofs of connexion is in the fact that the Egyptian document makes clear the meaning of an unintelligible Hebrew word, rendered "excellent things" without justification (see R.V. *mar.*) in xxii. 20. The Hebrew consonants here can be read as "thirty," corresponding with the "thirty" chapters of the Egyptian parallel (see the *Journal of Egyptian Archæology*, Vol. XII, Pts. III and IV, p. 236). As a matter of fact, the section of Proverbs, xxii. 17–xxiv. 22, does contain thirty sayings (*loc. cit.*, p. 235), apart from the introduction (xxii. 17-21). As the Egyptian document seems to be the original, we have here an interesting example of that borrowing from foreign sources which is so familiar to us in regard to Babylonian literature (e.g., in the early chapters of Genesis).

The *fourth* section of the Book of Proverbs runs from xxv to xxix, and is headed:

THESE ALSO ARE PROVERBS OF SOLOMON, WHICH
THE MEN OF HEZEKIAH KING OF JUDAH
TRANSCRIBED

This second "Solomonic" collection is somewhat different in character from the first. The form is not confined to the couplet, and there seems to be more of an attempt to group the sayings by subject. Thus the first seven verses of xxv deal with kings, whilst ten verses in xxvi deal with "fools" (3-12), the next four (13-16) with sluggards, and a little further on (23 ff.) there is a series of condemnations of the deceitful flatterer. The religious element is not so noticeable here. Some of the proverbs are identical with those in the earlier "Solomonic" section, e.g.:

Better to live on the corner of the roof
Than a house in common with a quarrelsome woman

(xxv. 24, with xxi. 9) (cf. similar phenomena in the Psalms).

The *fifth* section is contained in xxx, and is headed:

THE WORDS OF AGUR THE SON OF YAKEH; THE ORACLE

The character and form of this are peculiar. It begins with a skeptic's agnosticism concerning God (1-4), which is followed by an orthodox rebuke of this attitude in the light of revelation, and a prayer to be saved from it (5, 6, 7-9). Most of what follows is arranged in what might be called "foursomes" —i.e., groups of four things which are alike, and may be held to throw light on each other: four kinds of evil men (11-14); four greedy things (15-16); four mysterious things (18-19); four unbearable things (21-23); four wise little animals (24-28); four stately things (29-31).

The *sixth* section consists of the first nine verses of xxxi and is headed:

THE WORDS OF LEMUEL A KING; THE ORACLE WHICH HIS MOTHER TAUGHT HIM

This warns against sensuality and wine-drinking and commends the cause of the helpless.

The *seventh* and last section has no title, but is clearly marked off from the rest, not only by its subject—the praise of a virtuous woman—but by the fact that it is an acrostic poem, in which each of the twenty-two verses begins with the successive letters of the Hebrew alphabet.

In regard to the question of date and authorship, we know nothing of Agur and Lemuel. The ascription to Solomon of Sections II and IV is of no more value than the copious ascription of psalms to David; these titles were written by scribes at a later date than that at which the collections were made, and simply show what these scribes conjectured about them. In fact, the title of the second "Solomonic" collection gives itself away by using a very late form of a Hebrew word, the one rendered "transcribed," which occurs nowhere else in this sense in the Old Testament, but is frequent in later Hebrew.

That proverbs existed from early days in Israel we know; that some of them have survived in our Book of Proverbs is highly probable. But much of the material in the book is so strongly marked by an advanced morality and the doctrine of retribution, both of which are inconceivable before the great work of the eighth-century prophets had time to influence other men, that the collection is most likely to be post-exilic, when foreign intercourse also made borrowing much more likely. The position is in fact very much like that of the Book of Psalms. Of the collections, II is generally regarded as earliest and the Introduction (I) as latest, and the period from the fourth to the third century is the most likely for the present literary form of the book.

3. *The Book of Job* is best described as a dramatic poem, set in a prose prologue and epilogue. The dramatic movement of the poem, however, is of the thought rather than of the action, which is of the simplest. The misfortunes of Job occurring in the prologue are discussed by himself and his friends in three cycles of statement and reply. After a soliloquy of complaint by Job (iii), the speeches run as follows: Eliphaz (iv, v), Job (vi, vii), Bildad (viii), Job (ix, x), Zophar (xi), Job (xii-xiv) forming the first cycle; Eliphaz (xv), Job (xvi, xvii), Bildad (xviii), Job (xix), Zophar (xx), Job (xxi) forming the second cycle; Eliphaz (xxii), Job (xxiii, xxiv), Bildad (xxv and (?) xxvi), Job (xxvii. 2-6, 11, 12), Zophar (xxvii. 7-10, 13-23), forming the third cycle, though in this there has been some confusion towards the end, the final speech of Zophar having been amalgamated with that of Job. There follows an independent poem on wisdom (xxviii), and a closing soliloquy by Job (xxix-xxxi) in which he challenges God. At this point there is the intervention of a new speaker Elihu to whom no reference has been made; after a brief prose introduction (xxxii. 1-6) he declares his dissatisfaction with both Job and his friends (xxxii-xxxvii). Next Yahweh answers

Job (xxxviii-xlii. 6), Job making two brief replies. The book closes with the prose epilogue describing the restoration of Job's fortunes (xlii. 7-17).

The relation of the prose to the poetry forms the chief problem in the literary criticism of the work, and our interpretation of the meaning of the whole will partly depend on this. It has been claimed that the alleged differences between the prologue-epilogue and the poetical debate prove that the poet appropriated an early prose booklet on the sufferings of Job and used it as the text for his much later discussion.

There is no doubt about the post-exilic date of the poetry, and there may have been a prose narrative of Job's sufferings which was of pre-exilic date (cf. the reference of Ezekiel to Job in xiv. 14, 20); but the fact remains that even if the author of the poetry has not himself written the first draft of the prose, he had adopted and perhaps adapted it, and given it currency in the book as a whole. The debate would be unintelligible if there were no prologue, and the author has accepted the prologue as the sufficient explanation of the debate, so that he at least could not have felt differences of outlook to be irreconcilable.

We may conclude therefore that the prologue and the epilogue must be taken as essential to the ultimate purpose of the author, and our interpretation of the book must be based on this unity.

There is general agreement, however, that the speeches of Elihu are not part of the original poem. They interrupt the argument; they have no basis in it by any reference to Elihu in the poem or the prose narrative; they involve both repetition of what has been said by the friends of Job and anticipation of what Yahweh will say; the style and vocabulary are markedly different. But they do emphasize more than is done elsewhere the value of suffering as discipline. Most scholars also agree that the "meditation" on wisdom is a detached poem, though a very fine one, which has been inserted later. Some scholars also think that the second speech of Yahweh, including the description of Behemoth and Leviathan, are additions, though this is less certain.

The subject of the book is the suffering of the innocent and the prosperity of the wicked—i.e., the justice of God as based on the principle of exact moral retribution within this world. Job denies it, on the ground that he knows himself to be innocent of anything that could deserve such sufferings; the friends assert it, on the ground that God must act according to his principle, and that Job must therefore be deceived in his impression of his own innocence. The speeches of Yahweh simply amount to saying that the wisdom of God, as seen in the order and complexity of the world, are beyond Job's comprehension and that therefore he is wrong in denouncing God as unjust; to this Job finally assents. If this is all the author meant, then the book offers no solution of the problem it discusses; it simply tells men that they cannot understand God, and must be content to trust Him even when He seems to be unjust. But if, as we have seen, the author has made himself responsible for the prologue, then we are justified in saying that the veil of mystery which hangs over God's purpose for Job is here lifted. Job suffered to prove that disinterested religion is a reality; he unconsciously bore witness to the reality of such religion. This forms a distinct interpretation of innocent suffering, beyond the theory of discipline or chastening which is found elsewhere in the book. The disinterestedness of the service rendered is all the more clearly seen because there is no confidence in any life beyond death, since the mere ghostly existence in Sheol is not "life" (iii. 13-19). It is true that here and there we find a wistful and pathetic longing (xiv. 13-15) for some future vindication of the misjudged sufferer. But the only place where this longing passes into temporary confidence is in the famous words of xix. 25, 26, which fall far short in meaning of the Christian hope of life beyond death which their place in the Funeral Service gives them. We should rather compare with it the cry of dereliction on the Cross and hear in both something of what R. L. Stevenson has called "the half of a broken hope for a pillow at night," which makes the steadfast trust and loyalty of both the human and the divine sufferer all the more impressive. The highest contribution to the solution of the problem of innocent suffering made by the Book of Job is that such suffering may serve the divine purpose to promote true religion upon the earth, and all the more when the sufferer remains unconscious of the extent of his service. The disguise of the friendly God in the form of a foe recalls the *motif* of Jacob's wrestle in the darkness (Gen. xxxii. 24 ff.).

The date of the book is certainly post-exilic. It belongs to the late Persian or to the early Greek period, probably to the former, say about 400. This is suggested by the conception of Satan (cf. the Satan of Zechariah iii and 1 Chronicles xxi. 1, and also the Persian Ahriman), the angelology, the language, the character and treatment of the problem itself, the dependence on Jeremiah xx. 14-18 (Job iii) and Psalm viii (Job. vii. 17, 18). There is a Babylonian poem dealing with the sufferings of a king who cannot find out what he has done to make the gods angry, but it remains an open question whether this has influenced our "Job." The same remark applies to Egyptian discussions amongst the Wise Men.

4. *The Book of Ecclesiastes* is the third canonical example of the Wisdom Literature. It makes use of the name of Solomon as of one eminently fitted by his position to experiment on the values of life—very much as Goethe has made use of Faust. But the Hebrew of Ecclesiastes is of the latest type, and the background of misgovernment and oppression, of pessimism and partial skepticism, which is presupposed by the book, agrees best with a date about 200 B.C. It is possible that Greek thought has indirectly influenced the attitude of the writer, which is strongly opposed to the general trend of Jewish religion.

In form the book is an elaborate indictment of life, which shows the monotony of nature and history (i. 2-11), the helpless routine of human life (iii. 1-8), the failure to gain satisfaction whether from material (ii. 4-11), intellectual (viii. 16-17, and iii. 11), or moral (vii. 15, ix. 2) pursuits. Beyond the inconsistencies and disappointment of this life there is no other (iii. 19-21, ix. 4-5, xi. 8, xii). The writer can be described as both pessimistic and agnostic, but not as atheistic. He believes in God, but His ways are not to be known by man and the world order is full of injustice.

What contribution, then, can wisdom make to a

life so handicapped, where all is vanity in the sense of being empty and unsatisfying? (Contrast the different meanings given to the term "vanity" by Thomas à Kempis, John Bunyan, and Thackeray). The answer is that, after all, wisdom is better than folly (ii. 13, 14) and life must be taken as it comes, the best being made of it (ii. 24, ix. 7-9) with prudence and submission to the inevitable (viii. 3). Religious duties are to be discharged decently (v. 1-5), but here as elsewhere the motto is "Nothing in excess" (vii. 16-17). We cannot be surprised that such a view of life and of divine providence created great hesitation as to the reception of the book into the Jewish Canon. In fact, we may be certain that it would not have been received at all even though it was written in the name of Solomon, had it not been for certain scribal corrections of its heterodoxy (e.g., the appendix xii. 9-14, also xii. 1a, iii. 17, viii. 11-13).

Whilst it cannot be said that the book makes any real contribution to the solution of that problem of suffering which so engaged the thought of Wisdom writers, it is valuable to have this negative evidence as to the significance of Jewish faith. We can, in fact, see from the book just where "the Preacher" has left the main road of Jewish piety. He has divorced the present from both the past and the future so that he has no redemptive history or Messianic hope and he has also lost sight of man's social solidarity. On the other hand, God is hidden from his eyes partly because he neglects those values of life which bring a real knowledge of God. Christianity continues the highest development of Judaism in asserting that quality of life means more than quantity and adds to this (with post-canonical Judaism) that this higher quality of life is deathless. It is instructive to compare Ecclesiastes ix. 13-16 with the Christian interpretation of the Cross of Christ.

5. *Post-Canonical Wisdom.* Beyond the limits of the Canon the Wisdom Literature is contained in two important books of the Apocrypha, which demand brief notice here in order to bring out the significance of the Wisdom Literature in general. The first of these is Ecclesiasticus, written about 180 B.C. by Jesus ben Sirach and translated into Greek in 132 by his grandson, who added the preface. Almost two-thirds of the original Hebrew have been recovered in recent years. Ecclesiasticus resembles Proverbs in contents and outlook. It treats the topics, however, in a more connected fashion, though no definite plan of arrangement can be discovered. The religious outlook is that of contemporary Jewish orthodoxy with no consciousness of the problems raised by Job and Ecclesiastes, or of the hope of immortality as in the later Wisdom of Solomon. The

idea of Wisdom (e.g. xxiv) resembles that of Proverbs (viii) and does not show the influence of Greek thought nearly as much as does the Wisdom of Solomon. The book is specially interesting because of its glimpses of contemporary social life and moral standards. Note especially its praise of famous men (xliv-l) and its picturesque review of current industries in xxxviii. 24 ff.

The Wisdom of Solomon was written in Greek by an Alexandrine Jew, probably within the century before the birth of Christ. It is directed against both Jewish apostasy and gentile idolatry. Like Ecclesiastes, it uses the figure of Solomon (ix. 7 ff.), but in conscious opposition to the teaching of Ecclesiastes (Wisdom i. 10–ii. 20). The influence of Greek thought upon the writer may be seen in the Stoic doctrine of immanence (vii. 22 ff.), and in the Platonic psychology (viii. 20, ix. 15, xv. 8). The central idea of Wisdom as a divine power immanent in the world (vii. 22–viii. 8) identifies it with the Holy Spirit (i. 4-7, ix. 17). In the second half of the book (x-xix) the author reviews and amplifies the story of the Exodus in order to show the activity of Wisdom in the redemption of Israel, and deals at length with the contrasted folly of idolatry. The chief religious significance of the book lies in its solution of the problem of suffering through immortality and future judgment and its revaluation of life in the light of immortality.

6. The Song of Songs may be conveniently noticed here—though it does not belong to the Wisdom Literature—since its obvious interest in nature forms a link. The Song undoubtedly owes its place in the Hebrew Canon to the allegorical interpretation of it. Jewish exegesis made it a reflection of the history of the nation from the Exodus to the Messianic restoration, the key to that history being Yahweh's love for Israel. Christian exegesis, still reflected in the headings to the chapters of the Authorized Version, made it portray the relation of Christ and the Church (cf. Eph. v. 22-33). Both views are without foundation; the Song is of secular relations and is best described as an anthology of love songs. In the last century it was often held to be a drama with two or three protagonists (Solomon, the Shulamite, and sometimes the faithful shepherd). But too much has to be supplied to make this view convincing, and the analogy of the wedding customs amongst Syrian peasants at which bridegroom and bride play the part of King and Queen for a week, suggest that this is a collection of the songs sung on such occasions with other love-songs. (The occurrence of refrains suggests that there has been some loose arrangement of these.) In recent times some have maintained that

the songs were connected with the Tammuz-Ishtar cult, but this theory, like the "dramatic" view, demands too much imaginative reconstruction. Moreover, it is hard to believe that a liturgy with such pagan associations could ever have found its way into the Canon.

As a collection of secular love-songs in Oriental taste and sexual frankness, the anthology is of much beauty and interest, and gives us a glimpse of that lost Israelite literature which could find no place in the Canon. It was probably compiled in the Greek period, but some elements of it may go back many generations.

CHAPTER VII

THE LAW LITERATURE

In Chapter III, dealing with the historical literature, the Pentateuch was considered in its present form of a history containing a law, but the examination of that law was deferred for separate notice. In this chapter we shall trace the rise and development of the several codes of law which are a characteristic feature of the Old Testament.

1. By the "law" of a society we usually mean those rules of conduct which it prescribes and enforces by direct or indirect sanctions. Amongst ourselves, such law may come into being through an "Act of Parliament"—i.e., through the formal and definite act of the representatives of the society. But there is also the great body of "common law"—i.e., the unwritten law which judges administer and to which they are constantly adding by their own decisions. It is this element which links us most closely with the origins of law in the customs of a society. Before the society has worked out any representative system of government, and before it has attained the unity of central rule at all, it has its ruling customs which are the germs of law. Sometimes we can see

the occasion in which they began. When David was making a raid against the Amalekites (1 Sam. xxx. 7-25) a quarter of his men were left behind, and after the raid, a dispute arose as to whether they were entitled to share in the spoil. But David said, "As his share is that goeth down to the battle, so shall his share be that tarrieth by the stuff; they shall share alike. And it was so from that day forward, that he made it a statute and an ordinance for Israel, unto this day." Yet in Numbers xxxi. 27, this "law" is assigned to Moses (P) as part of the original revelation. This is an example of case-law, where the practice dates from a definite ruling on some historic occasion. But ordinarily the "laws" of a primitive society will come into being more or less unconsciously, without being linked with any one person or group of legislators. Who shall say when the "law" first came into existence, that ".Thou shalt not boil a kid in its mother's milk"? It may go back to some primitive taboo, or the milk may be regarded as blood, the phrase "mother's milk" being simply "goat's milk," still used by Bedouins for boiling flesh; the one thing it does not mean is a humanitarian regard for the mother.

Such primitive customary "law," unwritten and often only sanctioned by vague or definite superstitious fears, was not essentially connected with the

religion of a primitive society, itself not less vague
and ununified. But, obviously, as the society developed there would be the tendency to bring its public
"law"—that is, its accepted customs—more and more
into relation with its religion, and often to trace its
more advanced codes of law to the direct inspiration
of its deities. Thus the god Shamash is the inspirer
of the Code of Hammurabi. At the top of the stone
on which that law is inscribed, we see the Babylonian
sun-god seated on his throne, his feet resting on the
mountains, and flames rising from his shoulders,
whilst the king Hammurabi stands before him with
bared and uplifted right arm in the attitude of worship.

But long before we get to such elaborate codes as
this, or to codification at all, the god is thought to
inspire judicial decisions, as in the account of Moses
in Exodus xviii. 15: "the people come unto me to
inquire of God." Beginning with such decisions in
the nomadic life of Israel, accepted as precedents,
the subsequent written codes of Israel, with which
we are concerned, at long last came into being.
Doughty, in his *Arabia Deserta,* gives the best picture of the justice of the shiekhs, which virtually
continues the life of Israel's law-giver in the wilderness:

"This is the council of the elders and the public

tribunal: hither the tribesmen bring their causes at all times, and it is pleaded by the maintainers of both sides with busy clamour; and everyone may say his word that will. The sheykh meanwhile takes counsel with the sheukh, elder men and more considerable persons; and judgment is given commonly without partiality and always without tribes. This sentence is final. The loser is mulcted in heads of small cattle or camels, which he must pay anon, or go into exile, before the great sheykh send executors to distrain any beasts of his, to the estimation of the debt. The poor Bedouins are very unwilling payers, and often think themselves unable at present: thus, in every tribe, some households may be seen of other tribes' exiles.

"Their justice is such, that in the opinion of the next governed countries, the Arabs of the wilderness are the justest of mortals. Seldom the judge and elders err, in these small societies of kindred, where the life of every tribesman lies open from his infancy and his state is to all men well known. Even their suits are expedite, as all the other works of the Arabs. Seldom is a matter not heard and resolved in one sitting." (Vol. I, pp. 248, 249.)

When the Hebrews settled in Canaan, they passed from a very primitive type of life to one relatively of much higher civilization. We know from the abundant evidence of the prophets how freely the Israelites adapted themselves to that civilization in matters of religion, to such an extent that we can speak of a "Baalization" of Yahweh. In the same way, when they adopted the agricultural life of the Canaanites, the natural tendency would be for them to adopt the customary laws governing that life. No code of Canaanite laws exists to enable us to show the extent of this inevitable borrowing or influence. But we know that in the Tel-el-Amarna times (*c.* 1400 B.C.), Palestine was so much dominated by Babylonian influence that the Babylonian language was used for correspondence not only with Egypt, its titular governor, but even by local chiefs amongst themselves. It is probable therefore that Canaanite law was greatly influenced by Babylonian customs such as are reflected in the Code of Hammurabi. Thus (to take one example from many) Exodus xxii. 1 ff. corresponds with the eighth law of the Code of Hammurabi, though the fine is there greater (the community being richer), and inability to pay it involves death. (See further, Appendix III to Driver's *Exodus,* pp. 420 ff.)

The fundamental word for "law" is "Torah," an authoritative decision on some vexed question, as by an oracle, and the word is probably derived from the casting of lots. Each decision of Moses in the desert, acting as a sheikh, is called a "torah" (Ex. xviii. 16); Isaiah says of his teaching, "Bind thou up the testimony, seal the *torah* among my disciples" (viii. 16); the wise man says "forget not my *torah*" (Prov. iii. 1). But the word comes specially to denote the decisions of the priests, the original keepers of oracles, the depositaries of the traditional rules and customs in religious matters. This is recognized in Jeremiah xviii. 18: "the *torah* shall not perish from the priest, nor counsel from the wise, nor the word from the prophet." We have an instance in Haggai ii. 11 f. of the prophet going to the priest for an authoritative ruling on a ritual point; as Malachi ii. 7 says, "the priest's lips should keep knowledge, and they should seek the *torah* at his mouth." In all these instances we are dealing with *oral* utterances, without any thought of a written document which would make resort to a priest unnecessary. But naturally, in course of time, it became convenient for the priests themselves to keep a written list of precedents or customary rules, from which the legal codes of the Old Testament are in part evolved.

Another important word for "law" is *mishpat*, which meant originally a sentence given by a judge or *shophet*, then probably a custom based on such sentences or prior to them, and finally a "law" as a recognized principle of procedure. Here we have

a second source of "laws," and both are represented
in the collection of early laws known as "The Book
of the Covenant"—viz., ceremonial and moral
"words" and civil and criminal "judgments" (Ex.
xx. 22–xxiii. 19).

2. The central part of *The Book of the Covenant* consists of "judgments," actual decisions which
are recorded as precedents (xxi. 1–xxii. 17). With
two exceptions (xxi. 17, the cursing of father and
mother, xxii. 2, 3, burglary), these judgments appear
to be grouped in eight pentads, sets of five for mne-
monic purposes, dealing with the following:

Male slaves, xxi. 1-6.

Female slaves, xxi. 7-11.

Acts of violence, xxi. 12-16. 17 Cursing parents.

Personal injuries, xxi. 18-27.

Injuries by beasts, xxi. 28-32.

Negligence or theft, xxi. 33–xxii. 4; 2, 3, Burglary; 5, 6, Loss by fire (see Driver, *Commentary*).

Deposits, xxii. 7-13.

Loans, xxii. 14-17.

These "judgments," it will be seen, relate to civil
and criminal matters, and correspond generally with
the contents of the more elaborate Code of Hammurabi, as has already been indicated.

The rest of the Book of the Covenant is of a different nature, relating on the one hand to worship and the festivals, and on the other to moral and social evils in the prophetic manner. Thus we have:

xx. 22-26.	Prohibition of graven images.
	Construction of altars.
xxii. 29, 30.	First fruits. 31 (cf. Deut. xiv. 21).
xxiii. 10-19.	The Sabbatical Year.
	The Sabbath.
	The three annual Pilgrimages.
	Sacrifice.

and again:

xxii. 18-28.	Sorcery.
	Bestiality.
	Other gods.
	Stranger, widow, orphan.
	Debtors and creditors. 28 (cf. Lev. xxiv. 15).
xxiii. 1-9.	Evidence.
	Help to enemy's beast.
	Equity in judgment.

These elements of the Book of the Covenant may be generally classed as "Words" in distinction from "Judgments," and belong to the general class of customary rules ultimately going back to "Toroth" in many instances, or reflecting the general conscience of the community.

Robertson Smith, in an admirable characterization of the community for which this code was designed (*The Old Testament in the Jewish Church*, pp. 340-342), points out its simple structure, its agricultural occupation, its punishment by retaliation together with pecuniary compensation for injury, the rights of the slave, the inferior position of women, the absence of any central executive authority (though the tribunal of the sanctuary gives decisions), the sacred dues and their festivals celebrated at a plurality of local sanctuaries. Such conditions point to the period of the early monarchy as the date of origin of this earliest collection of Hebrew laws.

In what has been said the Decalogue (Ex. xx. 1-17; Deut. v. 6-21) has been left out of account. Some scholars still argue for a Mosaic original, however amplified, as by the "Words" relating to graven images and the Sabbath. But the general view is that this short code epitomizes the prophetic teaching of the eighth century. An earlier code than this may be the ritual "ten words" which seem to be embedded in Exodus xxxiv. 10-26 (see Driver's *Commentary* in the "Cambridge Bible").

3. *The Deuteronomic Laws.* We have already

considered the Book of Deuteronomy, apart from its legislative portions (Ch. III., p. 38), we have seen that the general style and the contents of the book, when studied comparatively, show it to be a distinct documentary source in the Pentateuch (p. 43); and we have noticed the great religious interest of the book as a whole, since it is a prophetic manifesto of (virtual) monotheism, humanitarianism, and the doctrine of retribution (p. 51). We have now to consider in more detail the contribution of its central part (xii-xxvi) and the place of this in the law literature of Israel.

These chapters contain upward of eighty laws, which are arranged in three main sections. The first (xii. 1–xvii. 7, except for xvi. 18-20) deals with the central sanctuary and its ordinances; the second (xvii. 8–xviii. 22 with xvi. 18-20) deals with the recognized authorities—judges, king, priests, and prophets; the third (xix-xxvi) contains a number of miscellaneous laws, admitting of no precise classification, and closing with a characteristic chapter which gives a liturgy of thanksgiving, makes provision for the dependent classes, and utters a final claim for obedience. It is probable that part at least of ch. xxviii, a chapter of blessings and curses, also belonged to the Code; there are similar conclusions to the Book of the Covenant (Ex. xxiii. 20-33) and the

Law of Holiness (Lev. xxvi). Driver, whose detailed comparison of the Deuteronomic Laws with these codes may be seen in his *Commentary* on Deuteronomy (pp. iii-xix), concludes that the Deuteronomic Code is an expansion of the laws in the Book of the Covenant, of which it may be described as "a revised and enlarged edition" (p. xix).

The outstanding religious qualities of the first part of the Book of Deuteronomy (i-xi) are continued in the legislative portion, so far as a code of laws allows. The monotheism expressed in ch. vi has for its legislative counterpart the law of the central sanctuary (ch. xii), the one and only place where the one and only God is to be worshipped.

The expansion of the earlier code is often in the enforcement of such humanity as the eighth century prophets had taught; we may take as an example the appeal to imaginative sympathy with the slave, the foreigner, the fatherless, and the widow: "thou shalt remember that thou wast a bondman in the land of Egypt" (xv. 15, xvi. 12, xxiv. 18-22).

The doctrine of retribution finds frequent expression in the warnings and threats of the Code, which culminate in the blessings and curses of ch. xxviii. Yet we must not forget that throughout the whole book the relation of Israel to Yahweh is based on much more than the hope of reward or the fear of punishment. The book borrows far more from Hosea than from Amos and urges love for God as the true motive, a love that is based on the "love-ableness" of God, as seen in His redemptive work (Deut. vi. 20 ff.).

The Book of Deuteronomy is of importance for the student of the Old Testament, not only because of its religious, but also because of its critical significance. Its central part, the legislative code which begins with such marked insistence on a central and unique sanctuary and adjusts earlier customs, such as the festivals or the support of country priests, to this drastic change, has been identified by most scholars in modern times with the law-book found in the temple in 621 (2 Kings xxiii. 1-24).

The reforms of Josiah included the abolition of foreign methods of worshipping Yahweh and foreign objects of worship, methods of magic and divination, the sanctuaries of rival deities, the high places of Judah, and beyond it, even at Bethel, and the concentration of worship at the one sanctuary of Jerusalem, where the feast of Passover was celebrated in accordance with Deuteronomic Law. Neither the Pentateuch as a whole nor any part of it, except Deuteronomy, would supply such a book as underlay this reformation. Whatever the origin of this book, we are therefore historically justified in treating its legislation apart from the rest, and this verdict on grounds of history is amply confirmed by a comparison of the contents of the book with the rest of the Pentateuch.

In recent times this critical position in regard to Deuteronomy has been attacked in two ways. Professor Welch would date the book two or three centuries earlier and would connect it with the religion of northern Israel, as a parallel to the "Law of Holiness" in the south. He argues that many of the laws in it seem to be of early origin and that, except in xii. 1-7, the concentration of worship might be not at Jerusalem alone but at Yahweh-sanctuaries anywhere in contrast with Baal-sanctuaries. In reply to these objects we may and indeed must admit the early date of many of the laws; any law-code is likely to contain much old material; but the point is rather as to the date and purpose of this *collection* of laws. Welch regards the passage (xii. 1-7) about centralization at Jerusalem as a later addition and understands the phrase "the place which Yahweh your God shall choose" as applying to local sanctuaries anywhere. But his interpretation of this phrase has failed to convince other scholars.

Hölscher would bring Deuteronomy down to 500 on the ground that it was never practicable to centralize worship at Jerusalem alone, that high places continued to exist after 621, and that the Jews of Elephantine (in Egypt) towards the close of the fifth century knew nothing of Deuteronomy. All that Josiah did was to purify worship at Jerusalem, and Deuteronomy is intended to be a programme for the post-exilic community. This drastic view, which involves other drastic changes, has not convinced scholars as a whole; nor has Kennett's attempt on other grounds to date the book shortly before the Return been any more successful. The identification of Deuteronomy with Josiah's Law-book still holds the field.

The importance of this dating for the historical study of the Old Testament can hardly be overrated. The Book of Deuteronomy shows us the profound influence of the teaching of the eighth-century prophets upon subsequent legislation, and prepares us to find an influence not less marked in the Psalms and the Wisdom Literature which confirms our belief that they also are substantially post-prophetic, though (like the legislation) containing earlier elements. We are also able to trace the influence of the "Deuteronomistic school" on the writing of history, as in the Books of Judges and Kings, where the style and outlook of the editors who supply the framework is clearly akin to that of Deuteronomy.

4. *The Law of Holiness* (Lev. xvii-xxvi; known

as H). These ten chapters contain an independent body of laws, which may be compared with the much earlier code known as the "Book of the Covenant." It begins with requirements as to sacrifice, making no reference to the first half of the book of Leviticus, which has treated this subject so exhaustively. The slaying of a sacrificial animal is to be regarded as a sacrifice, and all sacrifices are to be offered at the central sanctuary, blood being tabooed (xvii). The next three chapters deal with unlawful relations of sex (xviii, xx, these chapters covering much the same ground, and probably being doublets) and with the general regulation of the life of the people (xix; cf. Ex. xx-xxiii). The next two chapters (xxi, xxii) relate to the priests, and to sacrificial food and animals. Ch. xxiii forms a calendar of festivals, though a good deal of this chapter, and of the miscellaneous rules for lamps, showbread, etc., in ch. xxiv belongs to P, not to H. Ch. xxv prescribes the sabbatical (seventh) year of agricultural inactivity, etc., and the similar law of Jubilee, this chapter also containing material belonging to P. Finally, in ch. xxvi, we have a closing exhortation, similar to that which we have already found in the Book of Deuteronomy.

The reasons for separating this body of laws (apart from the elements of P) from the rest of the priestly work with which it has been closely incorporated are as follows: (*a*) There is first that characteristic from which the name "Law of Holiness" has been derived—the constantly repeated emphasis on the need for holy separation from all that is alien to Yahweh. Thus in xix. 2, "Ye shall be holy; for I Yahweh your God am holy"; or again in xx. 7, "You shall sanctify yourselves, and be holy: for I am Yahweh your God." The last sentence, "I am Yahweh," comes nearly fifty times within these chapters. A score of similarly characteristic phrases will be found in Driver's *Introduction* (pp. 49, 50), where it is pointed out that many of them are found in Ezekiel also. (*b*) There is secondly the fact that this Code of Laws is apparently self-contained, beginning as it does with general rules for sacrifice, and closing as it does, with the words, "These are the statutes and the judgments and the laws which Yahweh made between Himself and the Israelites on Mount Sinai through Moses" (xxvi. 46). (*c*) Thirdly, there are differences of subject-matter from the rest of P. The sacrifices named in H are the two earlier ones, known as the burnt-offering and the peace-offering; it has no reference to the sin-offering or the guilt-offering. In Leviticus vii. 22-27 (P), however, it is presupposed that animals may be killed for food without being sacrificed, whereas in the earliest times all slaughter was made sacrificial. Here in H the earlier custom is followed. (*d*) Fourthly, there is a difference of tone and point of view from P, resembling the humanitarian legislation of D: e.g., xix. 9 (something left for gleaners, Deut. xxiv. 19), 13 (care for dependents, Deut. xxiv. 14 f.), 14 (care for the deaf and blind, Deut. xxvii. 18), 34 (love for the stranger as for oneself, Deut. x. 19), whilst this same chapter contributes the famous second half of the whole law (which Jesus couples with Deut. vi. 5), "Thou shalt love thy neighbour as thyself" (Lev. xix. 18; cf. Matt. xxii. 34-40). It should be noticed that there are some portions of H in other parts of the Pentateuch—e.g., Leviticus xi. 41-47; Numbers xv. 37-41. As to the date of the Law of Holiness, xxvi. 38 ff. presupposes the Exile, and the general resemblance of both language and point of view to Ezekiel suggests that they do not lie far apart. This Code was probably framed in Babylon in the early exile.

5. *The "Legislation" of Ezekiel* xl-xlviii. This is in the form of an "ideal" reconstruction of the life of the community when restored to Palestine. It corresponds with the "supernatural" and "sacramental" emphasis of this prophet that he should describe a "New Jerusalem" and "Holy Land" of which the keynote is given in the closing words, "Yahweh is there." All the conditions are framed to

harmonize with this majestic presence. The sacramental people live in a sacramental land. Zion is physically exalted, the salt waters of the Dead Sea are miraculously sweetened, the sanctuary is geographically protected from defilement by proper isolation. "Holiness" is here seen in its (probable) etymological meaning as "separation", and this is expressed in the plan of the temple and all its ordinances, so that Yahweh may return gloriously (xliii. 2 f.) to the temple He had abandoned nineteen years before (x. 18, xi. 23). Many scholars think that there has been considerable expansion of, or addition to, the ritual laws here given, to bring them more into line with those of the Pentateuch. Jewish scholars found the differences perplexing, and one of them, Hananiah ben Hezekiah, stored 300 jars of lamp-oil for the laborious and lengthy task of reconciling them.

6. *The Priestly Law.* We have seen (Ch. III, p. 42) that the latest strata of Old Testament legislation roughly grouped together as the "Priestly Code" are embedded in what is formally a continuous history, supplying the general framework of the present Pentateuch. One of the objects of this history was to account for the great institutions of Israel, both its Law and its Temple ordinances. The covenants with Noah, with Abram, and with Israel through Moses have for their signs the rainbow (Gen.

ix. 16), circumcision (Gen. xvii. 10), and the Sabbath (xxxi. 13). But besides such brief statements, at certain points in the narrative larger or smaller bodies of Jewish law are introduced, doubtless at different times, since the method obviously lent itself to later expansions and additions. Thus the law of the Passover is naturally placed at the appropriate point in the story of the Exodus (Ex. xii. 1-20, 40-51). The ascent of Sinai by Moses is made the occasion of a much larger body of law—viz., that for the making of the tabernacle and its furniture and for the consecration of its priests (xxv-xxxi), which is followed (after incidents taken from earlier sources, viz. JE) by a practically verbatim repetition of the instructions in the form of a narrative of their execution (xxxv-xli). In these details the priestly writer has reproduced the plan and ordinances of the Jewish temple of a much later age, adapting them to the requirements of an ideal sanctuary.

The outline of the Book of Leviticus (Ch. III, p. 30) indicated that it was wholly made up of priestly law, of different origins and dates; these have suitably been placed immediately after the details of the tabernacle. The narrative of Numbers includes further legislation placed at Sinai, dealing with the service of priests and Levites (iii, iv), Nazarites (vi), the consecration of the Levites (viii), together with further rules for the passover (ix). A large number of priestly laws are included at various points in the story of the desert wanderings (cc. xv, xviii, xix) or of the sojourn in Moab (xxvii-xxx), whilst some of the narratives themselves are chiefly concerned with the laws of which they are made the occasion (e.g., xxxi, xxxvi).

It was characteristic of Hebrew "realism" thus to affiliate its ritual and religious ordinances and institutions to its history. The legislation itself is the product of a slow growth; some elements in it, notably the "ordeal of jealousy" (Num. v), and the use made of the ashes of a red heifer (Num. xix) are clearly "fossil" survivals of ancient customs in the later strata. But it may be assumed that the traditional laws of many generations took their present form in the "Priestly Code" somewhere about 500. It is probable that this was substantially the Code which Ezra brought from Babylon, and made the basis of Judaism and that it was already integrally a part of the Priestly Narrative, with which it is now so closely interwoven. At a subsequent date the narrative became the framework of the whole Pentateuch (see Ch. VIII), and gave the predominant colouring to the "Torah," as the revelation of God to Israel.

With the post-cononical developments of Jewish

Law we are not here concerned. But it should be noted that the interpretation and adaptation of the Torah in the hands of the Rabbis was ultimately (*c*. A.D. 200) codified in the Mishna, and that the further discussion of the Mishna found shape in the "Gemara" of Babylon and Jerusalem, the Mishna and the Gemara constituting the Talmud. Thus the latest development of the literature became the dominant element, whilst the Christian "reformation" of Judaism carried through by Jesus and His disciples went back primarily to the Prophets and their apocalyptic developments, from which developments Rabbinical Judaism separated itself.

CHAPTER VIII

THE CANON

So far we have briefly considered the legal literature of Israel without regard to its recognition as authoritative revelation—i.e., its canonization. We can now put together what we know of the process of formation of the Canon of the Law, until the full Torah or Pentateuch is reached, and note other significant points in the process of the formation of the Canon as a whole.

1. By "the Canon of the Old Testament" we mean that collection of the literature of Israel, written in Hebrew and Aramaic, which became authoritative to Judaism in matters of religion, and was taken over as authoritative by the Christian Church (though by it in the Greek translation known as the Septuagint, which included other books). The word "canon" is Greek, being connected with the word "canna," a reed, and denoting a straight rod or bar, then a carpenter's or builder's rule, then some sort of standard, and finally a collection of literature, sacred or secular, which affords such a standard. The books of scripture are canonical as being the authoritative standards of faith and practice. Inasmuch, then, as the Chris-

tian Church appropriated its collection of authoritative scriptures from Judaism, though eventually
adding others of its own production, and reinterpret-
ing the whole in their light, our enquiry into the
Canon of the Old Testament is an enquiry into the
process by which the Hebrew Bible became authoritative over Judaism. Here we must carefully distinguish between the history of the literature and the
history of the canon. The literary creation of a book
usually preceded its recognition as canonical by a
long period, and not all the literature of Israel has
become canonical, though all that survived from the
pre-exilic period was perhaps included in the canon.
The later non-canonical literature, known as the
Apocrypha, practically representing the excess of the
Greek Bible over the Hebrew, was recognized, at least
to some extent, in the early Church as canonical, and
was eventually accepted as canonical by the Council
of Trent in 1546, when the Latin or Vulgate version
of this larger canon was made authoritative. The
Reformers confined their authoritative scriptures to
the narrower Hebrew Canon.

The most striking fact about the Hebrew Canon
is its triple division into "Law, Prophets, and Writings." The Torah, or Law, consists of the Pentateuch,
the five books traditionally ascribed to Moses. The
Prophets include more than the English reader under-

stands by the term; they are divided into the "Former Prophets" (viz., Joshua, Judges, 1 and 2 Samuel, and 1 and 2 Kings), and the "Latter Prophets" (viz., Isaiah, Jeremiah, Ezekiel, and the Twelve—i.e., the Minor Prophets), making eight books of so-called Prophets. The historical books may have been included as "Prophets" on the theory that the prophets Samuel, Nathan, etc., would naturally write the history of their own times, or possibly because some of their utterances are recorded in these books. But the actual reason for these books coming next after the law in the Hebrew Canon is that in all probability they formed part of a continuous historical work, from which the Pentateuch was artificially separated. This is certainly true of Joshua, since the literary sources into which it can be analyzed are the same as those of the Pentateuch, and from a literary, rather than canonical standpoint, we should speak of the Hexateuch, rather than of the Pentateuch. Thus a quasi-authoritative character would already attach to these separated portions, and they would attract to themselves the writings of the Prophets proper, and borrow their name. The third part of the Hebrew Canon contains eleven "Writings"—viz., Psalms, Proverbs, and Job, the five Megilloth, or "Rolls," read at Hebrew festivals (viz., Canticles, Ruth, Lamentations, Ecclesiastes, and Esther), Daniel (not placed among the prophets—as in the English Bible—because the second part of the Canon had been "closed" before this book was written), Ezra and Nehemiah (reckoned as one work, as they became in the hands of the "Chronicler"), and Chronicles, the last book of the Hebrew Canon. Altogether there are twenty-four books, which reappear as thirty-nine by further division in our English Bible, as well as in printed Hebrew Bibles. Josephus reckoned the original Hebrew Bible as containing twenty-two books, but he probably arrived at this number by including Ruth with Judges and Lamentations with Jeremiah, the number twenty-two being preferred because it was the number of letters in the Hebrew alphabet. The Greek Bible varies in the number of books included in its larger canon, but in addition to the books of the Hebrew Canon in Greek translation we find usually 1 Esdras, Wisdom of Solomon, Wisdom of ben Sirach, Judith, Tobit, Baruch, and the Epistle of Jeremiah, 1-4 Maccabees. We shall confine our attention to the triple Hebrew Canon and notice certain points in the history of its development, though at none of them can we speak of canonization in the full and formal later meaning of the term.

2. The earliest point at which we can speak of the formal recognition of a body of written law is 621 B.C., when the Law-book discovered in the temple

was accepted as authoritative by king Josiah, and made the basis of his public reformation of the existent worship of Yahweh. It is true, as we have seen, that there exists an earlier body of written law, known as the Book of the Covenant (Ex. xx. 22–xxiii. 19), and that the narrative of JE (xxiv. 3-8) by its present order suggests that this book was made the basis of the covenant of Sinai, ratified with sacrificial blood. But, apart from the fact that this Book of Law presupposes an agricultural community, and could not therefore be suitable to Bedouin tribes until after their settlement in Canaan, we cannot speak of such a covenant, whatever it originally was, as the canonization of a body of literature in the ordinary sense of the word. The nature of the Book of the Covenant suggests that it is rather a private manual than a public code. The first recognition of publicly authoritative scripture of which we have independent evidence in the history is that of Josiah's Law-book, and there need be no doubt in identifying this with the central portion of our present Book of Deuteronomy. When we recall the brevity of the book read, its self-authentication by the information it contained, the strong impression made upon the king as to the consequences of neglecting it (which must have been forcibly stated), it seems reasonable to find the original Code of Law accepted by Josiah as authoritative in Deuteronomy v-ix. 7, x. 12-xi, xii-xxvi, xxviii, which must therefore have come into existence before 621. As the whole teaching of Deuteronomy reflects the work of the eighth-century prophets, we must assume that this book was composed sometime during the seventh century—i.e., during the reign of Manasseh, as a product of the prophetic reformers who could not then stem the tide of heathen reaction under that king. At a later period there was added a historical Introduction (i-iii; *c.* 600) and an exilic second Introduction (iv. 1-40) and Conclusion, besides other editorial elements. Thus was formed the first contribution to the future Canon of Hebrew Law, as distinct from other existent literature.

3. The second fact to be noted in the history of the Canon is traditionally dated 444 B.C. (probably this should be 397, the seventh year of Artaxerxes II, Ezra vii. 8). "They spake unto Ezra the scribe to bring the book of the law of Moses, which Yahweh had commanded to Israel" (Neh. viii. 1), and he read it to the assembly from a pulpit of wood, the people receiving the reading with every sign of reverence, and when they understood their neglect of God's requirements, of emotion and grief. On the second day they found in the Law-book the command as to the Feast of Booths, which applied to the very month in which they were, so they proceeded to celebrate it

as bidden. On the twenty-fourth day of the same month, they "entered into a curse and into an oath to walk in God's law, which was given by Moses the servant of God."

Unfortunately we cannot be certain as to the precise contents of this law as then formally accepted. The narrative of the reading of the Law in Nehemiah viii suggests that the Law read is that which Ezra has already brought with him from Babylon (Ezra vii. 14, 25). The impression made upon the people is of something new, for they weep when they hear it (*v.* 9). The account of the celebration of the Feast of Booths agrees with the Priestly Code, as against Deuteronomy. For in Leviticus xxiii. 39, we read, "on the fifteenth day of the seventh month, when ye have gathered in the fruits of the land, ye shall keep the feast of the Lord seven days: on the first day there shall be a solemn rest and on the eighth day shall be a solemn rest." In Deuteronomy xvi. 13 f. we read, "Thou shalt keep the feast of tabernacles seven days, after that thou hast gathered in from thy threshing-floor and from thy wine press." Thus in Deuteronomy, no fixed point in the calendar is named, and the feast is seven days, whereas the Priestly Code and the celebration in Nehemiah viii. 18 make it eight: "on the eighth day was a solemn assembly, according unto the ordinance." Moreover, the people live ceremonially in "booths," according to Leviticus xxiii. 42 ("Ye shall dwell in booths seven days"), whereas in the Deuteronomic Law nothing is said of this. So far, then, the suggestion is that Ezra read from the Priestly Code alone, perhaps only from its central and earliest literary portion, the Law of Holiness (Lev. xvii-xxvi). We have also, however, an account of a solemn covenant in the tenth chapter, and its details do not wholly agree with those of the Priestly Code. For example, the agreement that "we should not give our daughters unto the peoples of the land, nor take their daughters for our sons," seems to point to Exodus xxxiv. 12, and especially to Deuteronomy vii. 2, 3: "Thou shalt make no covenant with them, nor show mercy unto them; neither shalt thou make marriages with them; thy daughter thou shalt not give unto his son, nor his daughter shalt thou take unto thy son." (The Priestly Code has no such prohibition.) On the other hand, the "tithe of the tithes," paid by the Levites to the priests (*v.* 38), is in accordance with Numbers xviii, not with the Deuteronomic law of tithes (xiv. 22-26, 27, 28, xxvi. 12-15). On the whole, the evidence does not warrant us in identifying Ezra's Law-book with the completed Pentateuch. Even if traditions of Deuteronomic and other law were still operative, it is more likely that the new law was relatively a unity, such as the priestly history and code, than that it should have been such a varied literary compilation as the whole Pentateuch.

4. The third point of interest is the date at which the Samaritan Version of the Pentateuch was made, for that substantially agrees with the Hebrew Pentateuch, and shows that the present Canon of the Torah was then once and for all completed. Here there is unfortunately uncertainty as to the precise date. We read that Nehemiah expelled "one of the sons of Joiada, the son of Eliashib the high priest, because he was son in law to Sanballat the Samaritan" (xiii. 28). Now Josephus (*Antiq*. xi. 8), apparently referring to the same event, tells us that the name of the expelled priest was Manasseh, and that his father-in-law, Sanballat, made him high-priest of the rival temple on Mount Gerizim, which Sanballat built. But Josephus dates these events after the rise of Alexander. The evidence is inconclusive; probably we are not warranted in saying more than does Professor Oesterley (in general agreement with G. F. Moore)—viz., "that the initial act which tended, in course of time, to bring about a schism, was due to Nehemiah's action; and that what ultimately constituted the definite schism (i.e., the building of a rival temple on Mount Gerizim) took place about the middle of the fourth century." (*History of Israel,* p. 157.) Some time previously—i.e., between 397 and 350—the Torah

must have been completed, as it would hardly have been the same for both Jews and Samaritans if compiled after the schism. As to its elements, we have seen that a substantial part of Deuteronomy had been accepted as "canonical" in 621. But there also existed by that time a considerable body of non-canonical literature—early songs, and collections of songs, records of Saul and David and Solomon and other kings, Babylonian myths and patriarchal legends, stories of prophets such as Elijah and Elisha. In particular two great cycles of narrative had grown up in the northern and southern kingdoms, incorporating more or less of this copious material, the work of the Elohistic and Jehovistic writers respectively, the southern or Jehovistic being somewhat earlier in literary form than the Elohistic. How far these cycles extended is open to debate, but certainly as far as the end of the present Book of Joshua. During the exile this literary inheritance had been treasured and edited, the combined J and E were united with D and were continued, in writings, compiled from a Deuteronomistic standpoint, to the end of 2 Kings. After the recognition of the Priestly Code through Ezra's agency as an independent work, a new process of combination must have gone on, perfectly natural when we remember that part at least of both these bodies of literature had been accepted as authoritative. But the new Judaism as a legalistic community attached supreme importance to the revelation of the Law through Moses. Compared with this, the history subsequent to his death was of quite subordinate importance. The result was that the material of the present five "Books of Moses," the Pentateuch, was separated from the rest of the literature and given a unique place of its own as the Torah. Thus, from a literary point of view, there is nothing to separate the Pentateuch from Joshua, and we speak of the Hexateuch; but from a canonical point of view, a sharp and clear division was made at the death of the lawgiver, Moses.

5. The fourth point in the history of the development of the Canon is not reached until about 180 B.C., when Jesus ben Sirach wrote the important "Wisdom" book now included in the Apocrypha under the name of "Ecclesiasticus." In the forty-fourth chapter of that work, he begins his well-known eulogy of the great men of Israel, "Let us now praise famous men, and our fathers that begat us." He reviews the most striking personalities of the past, in such terms and in such an order as to make it clear that the greater part of the Old Testament lay before him as it now lies before us—Enoch, Noah, Abraham, Isaac, Moses, Aaron, Phinehas, Joshua, Caleb, Samuel, Nathan, David, Solomon, Elijah, Elisha, Hezekiah,

Isaiah, Josiah, Jeremiah, Ezekiel, the Twelve Prophets, Zerubbabel, Joshua the priest, Nehemiah. He concludes with a long description of the priestly ministry of his own contemporary, Simon. This list, and its order, makes it plain that the Law and the Prophets were read by him as they are read by us, and this is confirmed by his mention of "The Twelve Prophets" as a distinct collection. It will be seen that he refers to Nehemiah at the close of the Prophets, and this book does follow them in the Hebrew Canon, belonging as it does to the third division, the "Writings." But he makes no reference to the books of Ezra, Job, Daniel, Esther, books now included in the third part of the Canon. There was excellent reason for this in the case of Daniel, for this book was not written until some fifteen years after ben Sirach. The Book of Daniel itself confirms the impression made on us by ben Sirach as to the close of the prophetic canon, for in ix. 2, the author writes, "I Daniel understood by the books the number of the years, whereof the word of the Lord came to Jeremiah the prophet, for the accomplishing of the desolations of Jerusalem, even seventy years." This is sufficient to show that the Prophets have now acquired "canonical" authority. But the clearest statement of the position of the Canon in the second century B.C. is supplied by the Prologue to the Book of ben Sirach, written by his grandson about 132 B.C. From this passage we can see plainly that the triple canon already existed more or less, though the manner of reference to the third element in it suggests that this third part was not yet definitely rounded off. The translator of ben Sirach thus speaks of "the Law and the Prophets and the others who followed after them," or again of "the Law itself and the Prophecies and the rest of the books." The third part has not yet acquired a name of its own, but the Law and the Prophets are fixed quantities, canonical literature. How had the second part of the Canon, the Prophets, come to be formed in the period between 400 B.C. and the second century? The answer must begin by recalling the fact that the history of the canon is not the same as a history of the literature. Already in 400 there existed the four books of the Hebrew Canon which have come to be called "the Former Prophets"—viz., Joshua, Judges, Samuel, Kings. As the halo of antiquity broadened about them, they came to be of more and more significance, and after all, they were of close literary connexion with the earlier books, and could be regarded as books of authority, especially since the work of Deuteronomistic editors had enforced the prophetic doctrine of retribution and found illustrations of it in the history. But side by side with these, Judaism possessed the rolls of the prophets, the records of their activity in the name of Yahweh from the eighth century downwards, records due to their disciples or to themselves. These too were gathered and treasured, and pious hands brought them up to date by additions and corrections. Thus there emerged, side by side with the "Former Prophets," the "Latter Prophets," bearing the great names of Isaiah, Jeremiah, and Ezekiel, though much of both Isaiah and Jeremiah is of later date. There remained the prophetical books of shorter extent, which were transcribed together on a single roll, thus completing the four rolls. Slowly the process had gone on, as prophet after prophet proved his right to say "Thus saith the Lord," until the prophetic inspiration ceased, and the records of its past activity became therefore the more precious, and attained canonical rank. That this cessation of prophetic activity is a principal cause in the closing of the Canon of the Prophets may be seen from numerous literary references to it. Thus in Psalm lxxiv (belonging to the Maccabean age), there is the cry:

We see not our signs:
There is no more any prophet;
Neither is there among us any that knoweth how long
(v. 9).

In the First Book of Maccabees, we read that vexed questions were put aside "until there should come a prophet to give an answer concerning them" (iv. 46), or that "there was great tribulation in Israel, such as was not since the time that no prophet appeared unto them" (ix. 27), or that "the Jews and the priests were well pleased that Simon should be their leader and high priest for ever, until there should arise a faithful prophet" (xiv. 41). [There is a very late passage in the Book of Zechariah (xiii. 2-6) which pictures the utter disrepute into which prophecy had fallen: see Ch. IV, p. 126.]

6. The fifth point is the evidence supplied by the New Testament, taken in conjunction with two important passages from 4 Ezra and Josephus. The New Testament does not enable us to say that the third part of the Canon (the Writings) was formally closed by the Christian era, but virtually at least the Writings had become a more or less definite collection, to which appeal could be made for authoritative guidance. We may not infer this from the words of Jesus in Luke xxiv. 44, "All things must needs be fulfilled which are written in the law of Moses, and the prophets, and the psalms, concerning me," because the third part of the Canon is here represented by only one of its books, though the most important. But all the books of our present Old Testament are

quoted in the New Testament, except Obadiah, Nahum, Ezra, Nehemiah, Esther, Canticles, and Ecclesiastes. Now the first two are short prophecies and were beyond question part of the Canon in its second division a couple of centuries earlier, for they belong to the "Twelve" recognized by ben Sirach. As for Ezra and Nehemiah, their omission is quite accidental, for the Book of Chronicles which once formed part of the same work is quoted, and apparently in such a way as implies its present position in the Hebrew Bible—i.e., the last book of the Canon. This comes out in the passage in which Jesus speaks of the blood of all the prophets being required of the present generation, "from the blood of Abel unto the blood of Zachariah, who perished between the altar and the sanctuary" (Luke xi. 51; in Matt. xxiii. 35, "Zachariah the son of Barachiah," perhaps by confusion with the prophet). This seems to refer to 2 Chronicles xxiv. 20-22: Zechariah the son of Jehoiada testified against the people under the influence of the spirit, and they stoned him to death at the commandment of king Joash (835-796) and when he died he said, "Yahweh look upon it and require it." Thus the reference really amounts to saying "from one end of the Bible to the other," or as the Christian says, "from Genesis to Revelation."

There is clear recognition of the Book of Daniel,

which we know to have been written about 165 B.C. ("the abomination of desolation," Matt. xxiv. 15; cf. Dan. xi. 31, xii. 11). We must remember that this book does not belong to the Prophets, as the order of the book in the English version would suggest, but to the Writings, a fact which reminds us that the Canon of the Prophets had been closed by about 200, otherwise so popular and influential a book as Daniel would certainly have been included in the second part of the Canon.

We have more explicit confirmation that the Canon was closed by the end of the first Christian century in the contemporary evidence of 4 Ezra and Josephus. Ezra (xiv. 44 ff., *c.* A.D. 90) dictates ninety-four books, since the ancient scriptures are supposed to have been lost. God then says to him, "The first that thou hast written publish openly, and let the worthy and unworthy read it: but keep the seventy last, that thou mayest deliver them to such as be wise among thy people." The twenty-four books that are published are evidently the twenty-four books of the Hebrew Canon as finally accepted. Again Josephus (*c. Apionem* i. §§7 ff., *c.* A.D. 100) speaks of a definite Canon, which he enumerates as consisting of (1) the five books of Moses, (2) "From the death of Moses to the (death) of Artaxerxes, King of Persia, the successor of Xerxes, the prophets who succeeded Moses wrote the history of the events that occurred in their own time, in thirteen books; (3) the remaining four documents comprise hymns to God and practical precepts to men." This makes a total of twenty-two, and Josephus seems to have reached this number and arrangement by taking together the books he would call historical under the head of the "Prophets"—viz., Joshua, Judges with Ruth, Samuel, Kings, Chronicles, Ezra and Nehemiah, Esther, Job, Daniel, Isaiah, Jeremiah with Lamentations, Ezekiel, The Twelve. The four remaining books are the Psalms, Canticles, Proverbs, and Ecclesiastes, as we may reasonably infer.

In saying that the Canon of the Old Testament was *virtually* closed by New Testament times, we have to leave room for two groups of facts, not unimportant—viz., (1) that the New Testament does not quote from Esther, Canticles, and Ecclesiastes, whilst about these three books there was controversy among the Jews themselves; (2) that the New Testament does refer to certain non-canonical writings in a way that suggests there was no very absolute line in regard to the Writings. As to the disputed books, Esther, Canticles, Ecclesiastes, the canonicity of Canticles and Ecclesiastes was discussed and confirmed at the Jewish Synod of Jamnia (A.D. 90), and the whole present Canon seems to have been accepted. As to the use of non-canonical writings as Scriptures in the New Testament, perhaps the only quite clear case of their citation as authoritative or canonical Scripture is that of Enoch by Jude (14-16), which brings together several passages from Enoch (i. 9, v. 4, cf. xxvii. 2). Some Christian teachers (e.g., Augustine) argued that the apostolic quotation proved Enoch to be inspired; others (mentioned by Jerome) argued that Jude was not inspired because he quoted Enoch, which reminds us how differently the same fact may be viewed by different people. The reference shows that the New Testament does not limit itself rigorously to our present Canon, and that though there was a definite body of Scripture accepted by Christians as authoritative, it was not yet rounded off as sharply as it is for us. Besides, the echoes of many other apocryphal passages show the range of Christian reading, as the citation of the heathen poet Aratus (cf. also Cleanthes) in Paul's speech at Athens shows that this range was wider than the Apocrypha and Pseudepigrapha. (We might fairly ask about the quotation, "For we are also his offspring," whether (1) it is true because a heathen said it, or (2) because Paul said it, or (3) because it is found in the present Canon of Scripture, or (4) because it has the intrinsic quality of truth. The answers to these four questions will test and define any theory of inspiration.)

As for other references to non-canonical literature, an example may also be found in the Epistle of Jude, for his reference to the dispute between the archangel Michael and Satan for the body of Moses (whom Satan claimed as a murderer) is drawn from the Assumption of Moses. Hebrews xi. 35 seems to refer to the martyrdom of Eleazar and the seven brethren (2 Macc. vi and vii). In two places early Christian hymns seem to be quoted, and the former at least as Scripture—viz., Ephesians v. 14, "Awake, thou that sleepest, and arise from the dead, and Christ shall shine upon thee," and 1 Timothy iii. 16 (Moffatt):

> manifest in the flesh,
> vindicated by the Spirit,
> seen by the angels,
> preached among the nations,
> believed on throughout the world,
> taken up to glory.

Altogether, we are probably justified in saying with Sanday (Art. "Bible," in the *Encyclopædia of Religion and Ethics*, Vol. II, p. 571), that "the great body of the Church went on using freely the wider Alexandrian Canon, which admitted practically everything that was found edifying." In speaking of an Alexandrian Canon, however, no formal and definite contrast to the Palestinian must be intended.

The Canon of Philo, the typical and outstanding Alexandrian, agrees with that of Josephus. But the Greek Bible came to include translations of non-canonical books without raising the canonical issue at all. Thus these books came into wider use and acquired a canonical authority from Augustine's time onwards.

7. *The Present Authority of the Old Testament.* What significance has the Canon for ourselves? Are we to dismiss it altogether, except as the name we give to a classical collection of ancient books? It is certainly clear that the modern man cannot use it in the manner of the early Church or of the Reformers. The early Church regarded it more or less as a prophetic unity from which arguments against Paganism could be drawn for the truth of the Christian faith, since this had been so definitely revealed through the ancient prophets. The details of such argument often seem to us mechanical and trivial and contradictory to the historical meaning. On the other hand, the Reformers, appealing to scripture as against the traditions and practices of the contemporary Church, made the Bible the text-book of doctrine. This meant that they brought an already formed or forming system of doctrine and elicited proof texts of that doctrine from the Bible, again regardless of the his-

torical meaning, which for the modern student must be the starting-point of interpretation.

(*a*) The answer to the question must be confined here to the Old Testament, and this is the more justifiable because historically, as we have seen, the authority recognized in the Old Testament writings was gradually extended to their complement in the New Testament. We must begin with the Old Testament as a collection of literature illuminating the history of an ancient people. In the ordinary course of our experience that literature is brought to our notice as commended by the use and wont of the Church—i.e., that particular branch of the Christian Church which has figured in our education. In the first instance, no doubt, we accept without question this literature as having more or less authority simply because the Church has commended it to us; but this is obviously no adequate or ultimate ground of acceptance. It simply raises the further question, why did those who came before us themselves attribute authority to the scriptures? To ask this question intelligently is to be faced with the issue most clearly expressed by the Roman Catholic doctrine. The Council of Trent in 1546 defined the Canon and prescribed a particular version of it. To accept this decision as a revealed dogma is a necessary element in the Catholic faith. If, however, we are unable to accept such an answer to our question (even though we fully recognize the pædagogic value of corporate commendation of the scriptures), what is the alternative? On what can the Protestant base his acknowledgment of the authority of scripture? In reply to this question there does not seem any point at which we can stop until we get back to the intrinsic quality of the truth which the scripture contains. We need not shrink from the full acceptance of such a position. Truth can be sufficiently compelling to win its own recognition, and God does not require a testimonial from anybody when He chooses to speak. If it be urged that such a definition of the authority of scripture makes its test merely subjective, the answer should be clear; the record of the truth gained in the experience of Israel, like the truth itself, is an objective fact as much as any other fact in the worlds of nature and history. In the interpretation of the fact the subjective factor is involved, but so it is in all scientific and historical research. Perhaps the truest parallel is our appreciation of beauty. Who would venture to objectify the conditions and elements of beauty without regard to the subjective approach? The Reformers themselves partially recognized the duality of the objective and subjective factors in the final unity of revelation when they spoke of the inner testimony of the Holy Spirit which completed the testimony of the written word.

(*b*) In such recognition of the authority of revelation through its intrinsic truth, three important principles are involved which ought to win our respect as more venerable and far-reaching than the decisions of any ecclesiastical council. It is not possible to develop them here, for such development would be a whole philosophy of revelation. But they can be briefly indicated. (1) To hear the Word of God to us in the history of Israel is to assume that time is not the antithesis of eternity, but part of it, and that the actuality of living, with all its cost, belongs to the eternal purpose of God. (2) If God so speaks in and through human experience, man must be in some sense akin to God and man's consciousness a true, though limited, reflection of the divine. But this is a truth to which the Christian is already committed through the doctrine of the Incarnation. (3) Such a revelation through the intellectually and morally imperfect lives of men implies the same principle of "kenosis" or self-emptying on God's part as does the Incarnation itself. This principle applies both to God's original fellowship with the Israelites and to His subsequent revelation to ourselves through their experience by the continued activity of the Holy Spirit upon us.

(*c*) Such an attitude to divine revelation has the great advantage that it makes room for the different responses of different generations, and for the gathered meaning of the classical words as subsequently interpreted from time to time. Already in the Old Testament as it lies before us, we can see that post-exilic Judaism has shaped the ancient Hebrew literature to its doctrinal and religious purposes—e.g., by the theory that a complete divine revelation was given once for all through Moses. The New Testament follows on in this path of reinterpretation by giving to prophets and psalmists a greater importance than to the Law, and by testing all things in the light of the Christian Messiah. So (with lesser differences) it has ever been and ever will be. The dynamic quality of the original contact between human and divine personality is continued through all human experience, which can never cry "Halt!" to God. Both Jewish and Christian theologians have tried to hold Him to the written bond, but have always eventually failed. The Old Testament has done its noblest service when it has introduced us to its ultimate Author as one greater than all His works, one who is "for ever young," in a happy Jewish phrase. The story of the *making* of the Old Testament remains the essential guide to its proper interpretation, but the *meaning* grows with the experience of every interpreter who finds God in it and through it.

APPENDIX

CRITICAL ANALYSES OF THE SEPARATE BOOKS

I. THE PENTATEUCH

A. BROAD CLASSIFICATION OF SOURCES

(Neglecting minor sections)

GENESIS i-xix (J, P), xx-l (J, E, P).

EXODUS i-xxiv (J, E, P), xxv-xxxi (P), xxxii-xxxiv. 28 (J, E),
xxxiv. 29–xl (P).

LEVITICUS (P) (xvii-xxvi, H).

NUMBERS i-x. 28 (P), x. 29-xii (J, E), xiii-xvi [P (JE)],
xvii-xix (P), xx-xxv. 5 (J, E, P), xxv. 6–xxxi (P), xxxii
(J, E, P), xxxiii-xxxvi (P).

DEUTERONOMY (xxxii, Song, exilic; xxxiii, Blessing, 8th. cent.),
i-xxx (D with accretions), xxxi. 14-22 (JE), xxxii. 48-52,
xxxiv. 1, 8, 9 (P).

B. SCHEME OF GROWTH

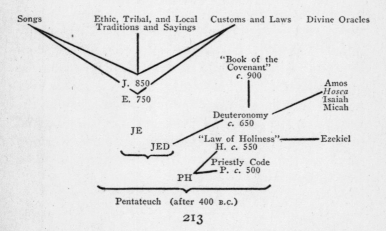

Approx. Date	Stories and Songs	Law (Oracles and Customs)	Prophecy
1100	The Song of Deborah. The Fable of Jotham.		
1000	David's Laments. Parable of Nathan. Court History of David. Solomon's Prayer. (1 Kings viii. 12, 13.)		
900	The Blessing of Jacob. (Gen. xlix.) (Book of the Wars of Yahweh.) (Book of Yashar.) Stories in "Judges." David-stories. (1 Sam. xvi ff.) Saul-stories. (1 Sam. ix ff.)	Book of the Covenant. (Exod. xx. 22 – xxiii. 19.)	Balaam Oracles. Micaiah's Visions. (1 Kings xxii. 17 ff.)
850	The Yahwistic collection. (1 Sam. iv-vi.)		
800	The Blessing of Moses (J). (Deut. xxxiii.) Stories of Elijah and Elisha.		
			Amos.
760	The Elohistic collection (E).		
750	Later stories of Samuel and Saul.		Hosea.
740			Isaiah. Micah (i-iii, vi-vii. 6).
701			
650	J and E united.		Zephaniah.
626			Jeremiah.
621		Deuteronomy.	
612			Nahum.
605			Habakkuk.
600	Deut. Edition of "Kings."		Baruch's Roll.
592			Ezekiel.
	Biography of Jeremiah.		
550	DJE, Judges, Samuel, Kings.	Holiness Code. (Lev. xvii-xxvi.)	Deutero-Isaiah.

(From prophecy there developed three lines of literature—apocalyptic, psalmic, and "wisdom"—after the exile, into which literature there were incorporated early mythology, psalms, proverbs, riddles, etc. "Lamentations" belongs to the exilic period.)

II.a. THE "FORMER" PROPHETS

JOSHUA.—i-xii. The (complete) conquest of Canaan. xiii-xix. Allotment of western territory. xx. Cities of refuge. xxi. Levitical Cities. xxii. Relations of eastern and western tribes. xxiii, xxiv. Farewell addresses of Joshua.

Indications that conquest was not complete (xiii. 13, xv. 14-19, 63, xvi. 10, xvii. 11-13, 14-18, xix. 47).

Continuance of JE (duplicate narratives: Deut. Editor in first half: P predominates in second, but not as framework).

JUDGES.—i. 1-11. 5. (Gradual) conquest of Canaan. ii. 6-xvi. Stories of early heroes, esp. Othniel, Ehud, Deborah, Gideon, Jephthah, Samson (Abimelech): six other *names.*

Theory of Deut. editor (ii. 11-23), *c.* 600 B.C. xvii, xviii. The Danites and Micah (Appendix I). xix-xxi. The outrage at Gibeah and its penalty (Appendix II).

1 and 2 SAMUEL.—Originally one book: divided by summaries (1, xiv. 47–52; 2, viii; 2, xx. 23-26).

1, i-xiv. Continuation of "Judges"; Samuel and Saul; duplicates.

xv-xxxi. Saul and David; duplicates; David's outlawry; Saul and the Philistines.

2, i-viii. David at Hebron and Jerusalem; the Ark.

ix-xx. The "Court History of David."

xxi-xxiv. Composite Appendix.

1 and 2 KINGS.—Four centuries; Deut. Framework of annals (didactic).

1, ii. Last days of David (from "Court History").

iii-xi. Solomon and his buildings (vi, vii).

1 Kings xii–2 Kings xvii. Israel and Judah (in parallels).

2 Kings xviii-xxv. Judah.

Sources:

 (*a*) Book of the Acts of Solomon (1 Kings xi. 41).
 (*b*) Book of the Chronicles of the Kings of Israel (17 times).
 (*c*) Book of the Chronicles of the Kings of Judah (15 times).
 (*d*) Prophetical Narratives of Israel.
 (*e*) Temple Records of Judah.
 (*f*) Biography of Isaiah (2 Kings xviii. 17–xx. 19).

II.B. THE "LATTER" PROPHETS

(1) THE BOOK OF ISAIAH

A. The "Book of Isaiah" resembles the Pentateuch and the Psalms in that it is a collection of writings extending over several centuries. These have been gradually added to the first roll, containing the prophecies of Isaiah of Jerusalem (eighth century), which are found in (*a*), (*b*), (*c*), and (*e*):

 (*a*) i. Short prophecies by Isaiah of different dates.
 (*b*) ii-xii. Prophecies relating to Judah and Jerusalem, chiefly by Isaiah.
 (*c*) xiii-xxiii. Oracles ("Burdens") relating to foreign nations, some (e.g., xiii, xxi) certainly later than Isaiah.
 (*d*) xxiv-xxvii. A post-exilic apocalypse, *c*. 300 B.C.
 (*e*) xxviii-xxxiii. Prophecies by Isaiah, all beginning with "Woe to."
 (*f*) xxxiv, xxxv. Post-exilic additions.
 (*g*) xxxvi-xxxix. Historical appendix from 2 Kings.
 (*h*) xl-lv. Deutero-Isaiah, the prophet of the exile (*c*. 550).
 (*i*) lvi-lxvi. Trito-Isaiah, a collection of prophecies of

different dates, but chiefly of the fifth century and in Palestine.

B. The period of Isaiah's prophetic activity (740-700) is that of the revival of Assyrian power in Western Asia, under Tiglath-Pileser III, Shalmaneser V, Sargon, and Sennacherib. The chief events that affected his teaching were the war waged by Israel (Ephraim) and Damascus (Syria) against Judah (734), the fall of Damascus (732), Samaria (722), and Ashdod (711) before the Assyrians, the revolt of Judah and Philistia, supported by Egypt, and the consequent siege of Jerusalem (701). During this period, the kings of Judah were Jotham (739-734), Ahaz (733-721), Hezekiah (720-693); from 734 Judah was tributary to Assyria.

C. The central thought of Isaiah is of the transcendent majesty of Yahweh, the Holy One of Israel (cf. vi), who desires from His people not the holiness of mere ceremonial (i. 11 f., xxix. 13) but moral innocence, justice, and humanity (i. 16, 17, v. 16). Isaiah's emphasis falls on the necessity of faith (vii. 9, viii. 17, xxviii. 16, xxx. 15) in spiritual, as against material forces (ii. 22, xxxi. 3). The symbolic names which he gives to his children (vii. 3, viii. 1 f.) denote his recognition of the power of the Assyrians, and his conviction that a "righteous remnant" (cf. vi. 13) would be left to Judah, after the divine judgment (cf. ii. 5-22), the laying waste of the fruitless vineyard (v. 1-7), and that this remnant (i. 25, 26, cf. viii. 16 ff.) would be established in Jerusalem (xxviii. 16-18, xxxi. 5), the inviolable dwelling-place of Yahweh (viii. 18) and essential to the righteous remnant. To this ideal future belong the "Messianic" prophecies (ii. 2-4, ix. 1-7, xi. 1-9, xxxii. 1-8), though their Isaianic authorship is uncertain.

D. In the sixth century the striking figure of Cyrus attracted the attention of a Jewish exile of unknown name, who hailed him as the "anointed" of Yahweh (xlv. 1), divinely commissioned to overthrow Babylon and to restore Israel to Palestine. The chapters now known as Isaiah xl-lv belong to the period of the successes of Cyrus in Asia Minor and elsewhere (xli. 2-4). The reasons why these chapters cannot have been written by Isaiah of Jerusalem are:

(*a*) Their presupposition of exilic events and conditions, quite different from those of the eighth century.

(*b*) Their characteristic ideas, such as that of God as the Creator (xl. 28 ff., etc.).

(*c*) Their style and phraseology, which are different from those of Isaiah.

E. The primary ideas of Deutero-Isaiah are:

(*a*) The "comfort" of Israel (xl. 1 ff.) through the promise of speedy deliverance, which rests on:

(*b*) The power of Yahweh over nature (xl. 12 ff.) and history (xli. 2 ff.), and His knowledge of the future (xli. 21-29). (Contrast the folly of idolatry, xliv. 9 ff.)

(*c*) A new conception of the mission of Israel as "the Servant of Yahweh"—a clearly drawn, individualized figure, prophetic in function, patient and gentle in spirit, conscious of being a weapon in the divine hand, and sustained by companionship with Yahweh, given the task of bringing the world to His feet, facing suffering in that mission, and at last victorious through the endurance of this suffering for others (xlii. 1-4, xlix. 1-6, l. 4-9, lii. 13–liii. 12).

APPENDIX

(2) THE BOOK OF JEREMIAH

A. *Contents.*

    (1) i-xxv. Prophecies chiefly about Judah, including some narratives.

    (2) xxvi-xlv. Narratives, including some prophecies.

    (3) xlvi-li. Prophecies about foreign nations.

    (4) lii. Historical appendix, taken verbatim (except 28-30) from 2 Ki. xxiv. 18 ff. (cf. Isa. xxxvi-xxxix).

The Greek text makes (3) follow xxv. 13, and conclude with xxv. 15-36; it then follows on with (2) and (4). It is in general much shorter than the present Hebrew text.

B. *The Compilation of the Book.*

    (1) The evidence of xxxvi; contents of roll of 604-603, which probably included much of i-xxv (largely autobiographical) and *some* foreign prophecies.

    (2) Additions made after 603—i.e., under Jehoiakim (d. 597), Jehoiachin (597), and Zedekiah (597-586).

    (3) A biography of the prophet, perhaps written by Baruch (xlv).

    (4) Addition of foreign prophecies, not by Jeremiah (e.g., xlviii, l. 1–li. 58).

    (5) The historical extracts from 2 Kings.

C. *The Foreign Prophecies.*

HEBREW: Egypt, Philistines, Moab, Ammon, Edom, Damascus, Kedar, Elam, Babylon.

GREEK: Elam, Egypt, Babylon, Philistines, Edom, Ammon, Kedar, Damascus, Moab.

D. *The Life and Times of Jeremiah.*

    Call, 626; disappointment with the reformation of Josiah (621); narrow escape from death (xxvi. 1 f.) for announcing destruction of Jerusalem; beaten and put in the stocks (xx. 2). In hiding (xxxvi). Imprisoned under Zedekiah, during siege of Jerusalem (588-586); permitted to remain with the Babylonian governor, Gedaliah (xxxix. 14), after fall of city. Carried into Egypt, where he rebuked Jewish idolatry (xliv).

E. *The Prophetic Consciousness of Jeremiah.*

Autobiography in i. 4-10 (call), i. 11-19 (mission), iv. 19, viii. 18 ff., xiii. 17, xxiii. 9 (anxious sympathies), iv. 23-26 (sense of Yahweh's power), xv. 10-21 (lonely sorrows), xx. 7-18 (divine compulsion).

(3) THE BOOK OF EZEKIEL

A. The priest, Ezekiel, was deported to Babylon in 597 (i. 1). He lived in his own house (viii. 1) at Telabib by the River Chebar (iii. 15) and was married (xxiv. 18).

B. He prophesied from 592 (i. 2, 3) till at least 570 (xxix. 17), and the exiles gave him attention (xxxiii. 30-33), but not response (ii. 5). His work was characterized by a strongly marked pathological element (catalepsy, with intermittent aphasia, iii. 15, iv. 4, xxiv. 27, xxxiii. 22), trance states (viii. 1 ff.) and many "symbolic" acts (iv. 1 ff., v. 1-4, xii. 1-20, xxxvii. 15 ff.).

C. His prophetic work was sharply divided by the siege (587; xxiv. 1 ff.) and fall (586; xxxiii. 21) of Jerusalem. This he constantly foretold, thus opposing the false optimism of the exiles (xii, xiii); but from 586 he was called to be a "watchman" and preacher of hope to the individual upright (xxxiii).

D. His book is mostly in prose, written by him on a clearly

marked plan, and frequently dated; the closing section on the temple seems to have been expanded by subsequent legislation. The first half (i-xxiv) is denunciatory of the people's sins, especially of idolatry; the foreign prophecies (xxv-xxxii) vindicate Yahweh's honour against Israel's neighbouring enemies (Ammon, Moab, Edom, Philistines, and especially Tyre and Egypt); there follow prophecies of restoration, including the notable vision of the valley of dry bones, and the "Gog" (Babylon?) prophecies (xxxiii-xxxix). The closing part (xl-xlviii) is a detailed account of the (future) restoration of the temple and the cult, which, like the companion vision of Jerusalem's idolatry (viii-xi), is supernaturally revealed to the prophet.

E. OUTLINE.

> i-iii. 15. Chariot-vision and call.
>
> iii. 16-xxiv. 27. Israel's sins and their penalty.
>
> xxv-xxxii. Foreign prophecies.
>
> xxxiii-xxxix. The hope of national resurrection, etc.
>
> xl-xlviii. Restoration of Temple (vision dated 572).

(4) THE BOOK OF "THE TWELVE"

First so called as group in Ecclesiasticus xlix. 10. Includes material from eighth to third century. Now the fourth "book" of Hebrew Canon. The order was probably intended to be chronological.

HOSEA (750-735).—N. Kingdom. i-iii; love for faithless wife reveals Yahweh's love for faithless Israel. iv-xiv; detached oracles against the priests and rulers, immorality (iv. 1 f.), idolatry and superficial religion; restoration of the really penitent (xi. 8 f.; xiv). Little interpolation, but text corrupt.

JOEL (*c.* 400).—Plague of locusts (i) as sign of Day of Yahweh (ii). Call for repentance (ii. 12-14), outpouring of Spirit (ii. 28, 29), Judgment (iii). (Transition of prophecy to apocalyptic.)

AMOS (760-750).—N. Kingdom. Judgment of all peoples, including Israel, on moral, not racial, basis (i, ii). Three addresses (iii-vi). Five visions of judgment (vii-ix. 8*a*). Later promises of restoration (ix. 8*b*-15).

OBADIAH (*c.* 450).—*vv.* 1-14, against Edom; 15-21, eschatological (cf. Jer. xlix. 14 f.).

JONAH (450-250).—A story about a prophet (2 Kings xiv. 25). Protest against narrowness of Jewish nationalism, in spirit of Second Isaiah (iv. 11). The psalm of thanksgiving is a later insertion.

MICAH (*c.* 702).—i-iii, against Jerusalem and Judah (cf. iii. 12 and Jer. xxvi. 18 f.), social and agrarian wrongs, sympathy with poor (Shephelah). iv. ff. Promises of restoration, etc., later than Micah.

NAHUM (*c.* 614).—Against Nineveh, shortly before its downfall in 612 (ii. 3-iii), now combined with acrostic psalm (i). Vengeance on Israel's enemy (narrow spirit, literary brilliance).

HABAKKUK (605).—i. 5-11, referring to Babylonians, should perhaps follow i. 1-4, 12-ii. 4, denouncing Israel's wickedness, on which the "Chaldeans" would then execute the divine penalty. Woes (ii. 5 ff.) and psalm (iii) later.

ZEPHANIAH (627).—The Day of Yahweh ushered in by Scythian invasion (cf. Jer.); heathenism of Jewish society; judgment of nations; kingdom of God.

HAGGAI (520).—Dated prophecies calling the people of Jerusalem to build the neglected temple. Zerubbabel as God's signet.

Zechariah i-viii (520-518).   Night visions; Yahweh's establishment of His kingdom; crowning of Zerubbabel (vi.
9-15).

ix-xiv (300-200).—Various prophecies of Greek period, often obscure and eschatological.

Malachi (*c.* 450).—"My messenger" (iii. 1); really anonymous.
i. 6-ii. 9.—Unworthy sacrifices and priests.
ii. 10-iv. 3.—Foreign marriages condemned; neglect
of religious duties; the coming judgment.

(FULLER ANALYSIS OF THE MORE IMPORTANT OF THE "TWELVE" PROPHETS)

Hosea

Hosea prophesied in the northern kingdom under Jeroboam II
(d. 746), Zechariah (746), Shallum (745), Menahem (745),
Pekahiah (737), Pekah (735)—i.e., *c.* 750-735.   His love for
his faithless wife (i-iii) revealed to him Yahweh's love for faithless Israel, and he penetrated more deeply than Amos into the
idea of religion as a right relation to God.   But, not less than
Amos, he urges right conduct towards other men as essential to
the true knowledge of Yahweh (iv. 1, 2, 6; vi. 6 f.).   He
especially denounces the Canaanite influences on the worship of
Yahweh, and the resultant immorality (iv. 12 f.).   His emphasis
falls on the love of Yahweh for Israel, His bride (ii. 19, 20), in
spite of her infidelity (ii. 14, cf. xi. 1 f.).   He is the prophet of
the decline and fall of the northern, as was Jeremiah (who resembles him) of the southern.

A. *Under Jeroboam II*

i. 2–ii. 1.   Israel's infidelity symbolized by that of Gomer;

her punishment and restoration; the reversal of the names of children.

ii. 2-23.   Israel's infidelity as Yahweh's bride; her punishment for turning to the Baalim; her restoration; the new betrothal and the new plantation.

iii.   Yahweh's love for the faithless Israel, symbolized by Hosea's love for and redemption of his faithless wife; the discipline and the subsequent return of Israel to Yahweh.

(ii. 2-23 is a *prophecy*, perhaps replacing a symbolic narrative like i and iii.)

B. 746-735

(There is little system or order in these prophecies of a decade; the meaning is often obscure, especially because the text is corrupt.)

iv. 1-19.   Israel's corruption, due to neglect of true religion.

v. 1-7.   Priests and rulers have misled the people.

v. 8-15.   The coming punishment; intended to produce penitence.

vi. 1-3.   Israel's return to Yahweh.

vi. 4-11.   The shallowness of the penitence; the depth of the sinfulness.

vii.   Wickedness of capital and rulers; deserved failure of foreign policy.

viii.   The vengeance of God, despite kings and idols, altars, and fortresses; coming absorption of Israel by the nations.

ix.   Sorrows of desolation and exile; due to false worship of Yahweh (Gilgal).

x.   Overthrow of Israel's altars and idols; the harvest of wickedness.

xi. 1-11.   Yahweh as Israel's father; unable to destroy utterly.

xi. 12–xii.   Israel compared with the ancestor, Jacob.

xiii.   Anger of Yahweh at Israel's ingratitude for providence (history).

xiv.   Israel promises to abandon other aids and gods; Yahweh's love.

Amos

Amos prophesied in the northern kingdom, though a herdman and sycamore-grower of the south (vii. 14), under Jeroboam II (782-743), c. 760-750.   He contrasts the zealous worship of Bethel and Gilgal (iv. 4) with the unjustly obtained luxury of the wealthy classes (iii. 10, 12, 15, vi. 4-6) and their oppression of the poor (ii. 6-8, iv. 1, v. 11, 12, viii. 4 f.).   Yahweh wants right conduct, not sacrifice (v. 24), and is stretching the plumbline of judgment (vii. 7) on Israel, which is destined to go into exile (vii. 17).   Amos also condemns surrounding peoples for various acts of cruelty or misconduct (i).   Thus he emphasizes the righteousness of Yahweh in His universal sway (cf. ix. 7).   The "Day of Yahweh" will be His intervention, not for Israel's, but for righteousness' sake.

Introduction

i. 1, Title and date; 2, the fundamental note of judgment (cf. Joel iii. 16).

i. 3–ii. 5.   The sins of Damascus (i. 3-5), Philistia (i. 6-8), Tyre (i. 9, 10), Edom (i. 11, 12), Ammon (i. 13-15), Moab (ii. 1-3), Judah (ii. 4, 5)—preparatory to the culminating attack (ii. 6-16) on the sins of Israel (social injustice and immorality); though Yahweh had displaced the Amorites for Israel and had sent His messengers to them.   Hence the coming Day of Judgment (overthrow in battle).

The Three Addresses

(*a*) iii. 1-8.   Israel privileged and therefore punished; cause and effect in disaster and prophecy.

       9-15.   Let the heathen look down on Samaria, and mark its disorder and oppression. Few of the wealthy will escape the judgment of war; sanctuary and palace will perish.

(*b*) iv. 1-3.   The luxurious women of Samaria.

      4-13.   Futile religiosity; the neglected warnings of famine, drought, blight, pestilence, slaughter, earthquake; let Israel prepare for judgment.

(*c*) v. 1-17.   The "dirge" of Israel; destruction in battle; Yahweh, not the sanctuaries, can save. The fruits of oppression will not be enjoyed. Do justly, and Yahweh will be gracious.

     18-27.   The woes of the true "Day of Yahweh," who scorns formal religion, and wants justice done.

    vi. 1-14.   The selfish luxury of Samaria's rulers contrasted with their coming suffering in siege. Moral perversity of Israel to be punished by invasion.

The Five Visions of Judgment

vii. 1-3. Locusts.

vii. 4-6. Fire.

vii. 7-9. Plumbline.

(vii. 10-17. Amos at Bethel.)

viii. 1-3. Basket of Summer Fruit.

(viii. 4-14. Greed, dishonesty, oppression, and the terrors of the "Day.")

ix. 1-8*a*. The Smitten Sanctuary.

(ix. 8*b*-15. (Later) promises of restoration and prosperity.)

APPENDIX

MICAH

Introduction. The undoubted work of Micah (i-iii, except ii. 12, 13) belongs to the period shortly before Sennacherib's campaign against Jerusalem (701 B.C.). Whilst referring to Samaria, he is chiefly concerned with Judah. A native of the Shephelah (i. 1, 14), he vigorously condemns the agrarian injustice and the urban evils, showing strong social sympathies. Yahweh will destroy city and temple, which are identified with this social injustice (iii. 12; cf. Jer. xxvi. 18, 19).

iv-v. 9 are exilic or post-exilic promises of consolation (iv. 1-3 appears also in Isa. ii. 2-4).

v. 10–vii. 6 resemble Micah's teaching, and might conceivably be by him, but the tone is different.

vii. 7-20 resemble many psalms and are clearly post-exilic.

Micah

i. 2-9. The Judgment of Israel.

i. 10-16. The Dirge on Israel's Downfall.

ii. 1-11. Social Injustice and its penalty.

iii. 1-8. The Unjust Rulers and False Judges of Judah.

iii. 9-12. False Confidence issuing in the Destruction of Jerusalem.

Exilic or Post-exilic

ii. 12, 13. A Promise of Restoration.

iv. 1-5. Jerusalem, Metropolis of the World's Religion.

iv. 6-v. 1. Exile and Restoration: Israel's Victory over the Nations.

v. 2-9. Messianic Anticipations.

vii. 7-20. Israel's Confession of Faith.

Uncertain

v. 10-15. The Purging of Israel.

vi. 1-8. Popular *v.* Prophetic Religion.

vi. 9-16.   Commercial Dishonesty and its Punishment.

vii. 1-6.   Contemporary Violence, Corruption, and Disloyalty.

HAGGAI AND ZECHARIAH I-VIII

(1) HAGGAI i. 1-11, 520 B.C. 1st day of 6th month.

> (*a*) Rebuke and appeal; disaster due to neglect of temple.

> (i. 12-15, 520.   (*b*) 24th day of 6th month.   The response to the message.)

(2) ii. 1-9, 21st day of 7th month.

> Promise of greater glory for second temple than for first.

> > (1) ZECHARIAH i. 1-6, 8th month.
> > Call to repentance.

(3) HAGGAI ii. 10-19, 24th day of 9th month.

> Past adversity due to contagion of irreligion; prosperity now at hand.

(4) ii. 20-23, 24th day of 9th month.

> Zerubbabel God's signet.

> > (2) ZECHARIAH i. 7—vi. 8.
> > The night visions.

i. 7-17.   The horsemen; no sign of crisis.

i. 18-21.   Four horns cast down by four smiths.

ii. 1-13.   The city without walls.

iii. 1-10.   The acquittal of Joshua (Israel).

iv. 1-14.   Candlestick and two olive trees (Joshua and Zerubbabel).

v. 1-4.   The flying roll; curse on evil.

v. 5-11. . Woman in ephah; guilt removed.

vi. 1-8.   Mission of the chariots; judgment upon the heathen.

(vi. 9-15: incident of the crowns; prince and priest.)

(3) ZECHARIAH vii, viii, 518 B.C. 4th day of 9th month.

Are the fast days of the exile still to be kept? Encouragement, if the moral demands of Yahweh be fulfilled; the happy future.

DEUTERO-ZECHARIAH   (Greek Period: after 331)

ix. 1-8. The Recovery of Palestine.

ix. 9-17. The Messianic King; restoration of Israel victorious over Greeks.

x. 1-12. Overthrow of the (foreign) shepherds and restoration.

xi. 1-3. Lament over fall of heathen rulers (shepherds).

xi. 4-14. The worthy "shepherd" rejected.

xi. 15-17. The worthless shepherd and his doom.

xiii. 7-9. Destruction of the worthless shepherd and two-thirds of his flock; the purified third.

xii. 1-14. Judah for and against Jerusalem: overthrow of enemies mourning for the pierced martyr.

xiii. 1-6. Cleansing of Jerusalem from idolatry and prophecy.

xiv. Jerusalem delivered from the heathen and made the metropolis of religion.

MALACHI   c. 450

i. 1-5. Yahweh's love for Israel seen in fate of Edom.

i. 6-14. Yahweh dishonoured through unworthy sacrifices.

ii. 1-9. The Priests have broken the covenant of Levi.

ii. 10-16. Divorce of native wives and marriage with foreigners.

ii. 17–iii. 6. Moral indifference and unbelief; coming judgment.

iii. 7-12. Prosperity dependent on payment of tithe.

iii. 13–iv. 3. Discrimination between ungodly and godly.

iv. 4-6. Moses and Elijah.

III. THE HAGIOGRAPHA

Miscellaneous character of this collection of writings, liturgical hymns and devotional poetry, love songs, gnomic, and speculative "Wisdom" stories, apocalyptic, and history.

These were collected between 200 B.C. and the Christian era; some of the books contain pre-exilic elements, but they are mostly post-exilic.

1. PSALMS. A collection of collections (500-100 B.C.; pre-exilic psalms).
   - i. "David," i–xli.
   - ii. "Korah," xlii-xlix (Elohim).
     "David," li–lxxii (Elohim) (lxxii Solomon).
   - iii. "Asaph" (1) lxxiii–lxxxiii (Elohim).
     Various, lxxxiv–lxxxix (Korah, David, Heman, Ethan).
   - iv. and v. Pss. xc–cvi, cvii–cl. Largely anonymous and liturgical: "Hallelujah" (civ. ff.), "Pilgrim" (cxx–cxxxiv).

II. PROVERBS. Also a collection of collections (c. 400–200 B.C.).
   - i. Introduction on Wisdom (latest part), i–ix.
   - ii. "Solomonic" collection (earliest?), x–xxii. 16.
   - iii. "Words of the Wise," xxii. 17–xxiv. 22.
     "Also of the Wise," xxiv. 23, 34.
   - iv. Second "Solomonic" collection, xxv–xxix.
   - v. "Words of Agur" and some riddles, xxx.
   - vi. "Words of King Lemuel," xxxi. 1-9.
   - vii. Acrostic poem in praise of the virtuous woman, xxxi. 10-31.

III. JOB. c. 400 with later additions (Elihu).
   - i. Prologue in prose, i, ii.
   - ii. Discussions of the problem of suffering in three cycles of conversation (poetry), iii–xiv, xv–xxi, xxii–xxxi.

  iii. Speeches of Elihu (poetry), xxxii–xxxvii.

  iv. Speeches of Yahweh (poetry), xxxviii–xlii. 6.

   v. Epilogue in prose, xlii. 7-17.

IV. MEGILLOTH.

Canticles: anthology of poems about sexual love (Greek period, but including traditional marriage songs).

Ruth: story of the Moabite ancestress of David; possibly against Jewish nationalism.

Lamentations: four acrostic poems, with a fifth, all on the fall of Jerusalem and written in sixth century.

Ecclesiastes: a "Wisdom" indictment of life, *c.* 200 B.C.

Esther: a nationalistic story of the origin of "Purim" (100–50 B.C.).

V. DANIEL.

(1) Didactic stories, i-vi (identity of the four empires in ii and vii).

(2) Apocalyptic, vii-xii.

(3) Evidence for the Maccabean date (*c.* 165 B.C.): position in third part of Hebrew Bible, language, ignorance of the sixth-century history; point at which the review becomes prediction.

(4) The characteristic doctrines:

  (*a*) The Kingdom of God.

  (*b*) The Resurrection.

  (*c*) Angelology.

VI. EZRA, NEHEMIAH, CHRONICLES.

Ezra and Nehemiah contain "memoirs" of the fifth century and other documents. The Chronicler (250 B.C.) edited them and prefixed his own ecclesiastical version of the history of Judah from the beginning (genealogies).

SYNOPSIS OF THE CHIEF LINES OF DEVELOPMENT

History	Prophecy and Apocalyptic	Devotional and Wisdom Literature	Law Literature	Religion
A. EARLY HISTORY I. Migrations. II. Exodus. III. Settlement in Canaan. IV. Saul and the Philistines. B. KINGS OF ISRAEL AND JUDAH I. David. II. Solomon. III. Warring Kingdoms. IV. Allied Kingdoms. V. Dynasty of Jehu. VI. Decline and Fall of Israel. VII. Survival of Judah. VIII. Fall of Judah.	A. PROPHETS OF ISRAEL Amos. Hosea. Isaiah. Micah. Zephaniah. Nahum. Jeremiah. Habakkuk.		LAW LITERATURE I. (Early Semitic) Hammurabi. II. Book of the Covenant. III. Deuteronomy.	A. EARLY RELIGION I. Nomadic Animism. II. Yahwism. III. Canaan. IV. "Pre-prophetic" Worship and Priests. Early Prophecy. JE Stories. Myths of Man and World. B. RELIGIOUS IDEAS OF OLD TESTAMENT* I. History as Source of Ideas. II. Idea of Religion. III. Idea of God. IV. Idea of Man. V. Approach of God to Man. VI. Approach of Man to God.

C. FOUNDATIONS OF JUDAISM		A. BOOK OF PSALMS	IV. Law of Holiness.	VII. Problems of Sin and Suffering.
I. Exile.	Ezekiel.		V. Ezekiel xl- xlviii.	VIII. Hope of the Nation.
II. Cyrus and the Return.	Deut.-Isaiah.			
III. Temple rebuilt.	Haggai.		VI. Priestly Law.	
IV. Nehemiah and Ezra.	Zechariah.			
V. Jews and Samaritans.	Obadiah.			
	Malachi.			
	Trito-Isaiah.	B. WISDOM		
D. FROM NEHEMIAH TO MACCABEES	Joel.	Proverbs.		
	Deut.-Zechariah.	Job.		
	B. APOCALYPTIC		VII. Canon of Old Testament.	IX. Permanent Value of the Old Testament.
E. MACCABEAN REBELLION	Isa. xxiv-xxvii.	Ecclesiastes.	VIII. Rabbinic Law.	
	Daniel.	Ecclesiasticus.		
	Eth. Enoch.	Wisdom of Solomon.		

(* The following headings are those of the chapters in the author's book bearing this title.)

233

SOME BOOKS DEALING WITH OLD TESTAMENT "INTRODUCTION"

J. E. Carpenter and G. Harford-Battersby: *The Hexateuch*, 1900.

K. Budde: *Geschichte der althebraischen Litteratur*, 1909.

A. T. Chapman: *An Introduction to the Pentateuch*, 1911.

*S. R. Driver: *Introduction to the Literature of the Old Testament*, 1913.

G. B. Gray: *A Critical Introduction to the Old Testament*, 1913.

G. F. Moore: *Literature of the Old Testament*, 1913.

*D. C. Simpson: *Pentateuchal Criticism*, 1914.

E. Sellin: *Introduction to the Old Testament*, 1923. Translation of ed. 3; last German ed. 1933.)

P. C. Sand: *The Literary Genius of the Old Testament*, 1924.

C. F. Kent: *The Growth and Contents of the Old Testament*, 1926.

J. Battersby Harford: *Since Wellhausen*, 1926.

J. Meinhold: *Einführung in das Alte Testament*, 1932.

* J. E. McFadyen: *Introduction to the Old Testament*, 1932.

D. B. Macdonald: *The Hebrew Literary Genius*, 1933.

J. Hempel: *Die Althebraische Literatur*, 1930-34.

*Oesterley and Robinson: *An Introduction to the Books of the Old Testament*, 1934.

O. Eissfeldt: *Einleitung in das Alte Testament*, 1934.

O. Weber: *Bibelkunde des Alten Testaments* (2 vols.), 1935.

S. A. Cook: *The Old Testament Reinterpretation*, 1936.

* These are likely to be most useful to the readers of this book.

INDEX

(a) SUBJECTS

INDEX

Joshua, 50, 52, 55, 57, 62, 199; Book of, 20, 34, 52, 54, 190, 197 f., 200, 205

Josiah, 43, 192, 199; reformation of, 43 f., 71, 178, 191 f.

Judaism, 112, 133, 141, 187 ff.

Judges, Book of, 20, 34, 52 ff., 58, 65, 180, 190 f., 200, 205

Judith, Book of, 80, 191

Kinah rhythm, 145

Kings, Books of, 20 f., 34, 52 ff., 65-67, 72 f., 77, 94, 180, 190, 197, 200, 205

Korah psalms, 138

Lamentations, 145 f., 190 f., 205

Law, canon of the, 188 ff.; codes, 26, 34; literature, 167-187; Psalms, 144

"Law, The," 20, 82, 88, 189, 200, 212

Legends, patriarchal, 47 f., 197

Lemuel, 154

Leviticus, 37 f., 40, 43, 180 f., 185 f.

Liturgy, 121, 138, 166, 176

Maccabean age, 19, 30, 144, 201, 202; revolt, 81, 132

1 Maccabees, 68

1-4 Maccabees, 191

Malachi, Book of, 118 f., 125

Manasseh, 86, 89, 100, 193

Megilloth, 21, 78, 190

Messianic hope, 117, 128, 162 f.; prince, 102, 115, 117 f.; Psalms, 143

Micah, 50, 89, 93 f.; Book of, 93 f.

Micaiah, 27

Midrash of Books of Kings, 77

Mishna, 187

Mishpat, 172 f.

Moabite stone, 31

Monotheism, 50, 114, 126 f., 141, 176

Moses, 16, 22, 34, 38 f., 41, 49, 51, 119, 130, 136 f., 168 f., 171 f., 182, 184 f., 189 f., 198, 204 f.,

207, 212; Assumption of, 207; Books of, 198, 204; law of, 202

Music, Hebrew, 135 f.

Mythology, 45 f., 100, 130, 142; Babylonian, 46, 142, 197

Nahum, 86, 89, 102; Book of, 102 f., 203

Nationalism, 13, 16, 80

Nature psalms, 141 f.

Nehemiah, 71, 74-79, 119, 122, 126, 196 f., 199, 205; Book of, 21, 34, 71, 75-77, 131, 191, 199, 203; memoirs of, 77

New Testament, 22; bearing on canon, 202 ff.

New Year's Festival, 143

Nineveh, 79, 101-103; fall of, 86

Nomadic religion, 68

Numbers, 38, 43, 185 f.

Obadiah, Book of, 119, 121, 203

Oracle, 171

Oracles, Book of, 96 f.; priestly, 26; prophetic, 26 f.

Oral tradition, 23 ff.

P., 42 f., 44 f., 51, 54, 168, 181 f.

Passover, celebrated by Josiah, 178

Pentateuch, 20, 34, 36-52, 54 f., 58, 67, 167 ff., 176, 178, 183, 188 ff.; value of, 45

Persian influence, 132; period, 86, 90, 116, 119, 125, 160; words in Daniel, 131

Pilgrim psalms, 138, 144

Poetry, Hebrew, 28 f., 135 f.; early Hebrew, 25

Priestly code, 112, 181 f., 184 f., 186, 194 f., 197 f.; history, 51 f.; law, 77, 112, 184-187; narrative, 42 f., writer, 43 f., 58, 60

Priests, 148, 172

Prophecy, 82-129; and Apocalyptic, 129 f.; and history, 132; contribution to religion of Israel, 126-129; decline of, 116-126; ecstatic,

237

INDEX

(b) SCRIPTURE REFERENCES

241

INDEX

243

INDEX

(The Appendix is not indexed.)